IMAGES
of America

THE NORTH
SHORE LINE

IMAGES
of America

THE NORTH
SHORE LINE

David Sadowski

ARCADIA
PUBLISHING

Copyright © 2023 by David Sadowski
ISBN 978-1-4671-0896-6

Published by Arcadia Publishing
Charleston, South Carolina

Printed in the United States of America

Library of Congress Control Number: 2022948572

For all general information, please contact Arcadia Publishing:
Telephone 843-853-2070
Fax 843-853-0044
E-mail sales@arcadiapublishing.com
For customer service and orders:
Toll-Free 1-888-313-2665

Visit us on the Internet at www.arcadiapublishing.com

This book is dedicated to the memory of Jeffrey L. Wien (1941–2021), longtime friend, mentor, photographer, and archivist, who worked for the North Shore Line in 1961 as a ticket agent.

CONTENTS

ACKNOWLEDGMENTS

The author wishes to thank the following individuals, without whose assistance this book would not have been possible: Bill Becwar, Marty Bernard, LeRoy Blommaert, Eric Bronsky, Douglas Davidson, John V. Engleman, Raymond DeGroote Jr., Kevin and Robert Heinlein, Frank Hicks, Nick Jenkins, Diana L. Koester, Genie Lemieux, Jim Martin, Marco Moerland, David A. Myers Jr., Ed Oslowski, Scott Patrick, the late Don Ross, Larry Sakar, J.J. Sedelmaier, David Stanley, and the late Jeffrey L. Wien. Special thanks go out to my editor, Stacia Bannerman. Unless otherwise noted, all images are from the author's collection.

Useful references for this work include the following:

Bulletin No. 106: Interurban to Milwaukee. Chicago: Central Electric Railfans' Association, 1962.

Bulletin No. 107: Route of the Electroliners. Chicago: Central Electric Railfans' Association, 1963.

Bulletin No. 141: Before the North Shore Line. Chicago: Central Electric Railfans' Association, 2008.

Anderson, Robert L. Grade Separation Project at Winnetka, Illinois. Evanston, Illinois: Northwestern University, 1941.

Campbell, George V. North Shore Line Memories. Glendale, California: Interurban Press, 1980.

DeRouin, Edward M. North Shore Line Interurban Freight. LaFox, Illinois: Pixels Publishing, 2005.

For further reading, check out the author's transit blog at www.thetrolleydodger.com.

Note that Chicago's street numbering system, in use since the early 1900s, is in the form of a grid, with State Street being the east-west coordinate and Madison Street the north-south. The numbers provided in parentheses after many of the street names will help readers orient themselves to various locations. For example, Western Avenue is 2400 West, which is three miles west of State Street, as there are eight blocks in a mile throughout most of the city.

INTRODUCTION

The Chicago North Shore & Milwaukee Railroad (also known as the North Shore Line) is long gone but has certainly not been forgotten. As we approach the 60th anniversary of its abandonment, there is a large and growing North Shore Line fan base. Many of these fans were not even born yet when the line quit.

The North Shore Line story came to an end on a very frigid January 21, 1963, morning. It began 70 years earlier during the Panic of 1893, which plunged America into a depression lasting four long years.

The Chicago & North Western Railroad (C&NW) extended passenger service north from Chicago in the mid-1850s. Where railroads went, goods, services, and people followed. By 1890, several communities between Evanston and Lake Bluff were known as North Shore suburbs, including Wilmette, Kenilworth, Winnetka, Glencoe, Highland Park, Highwood, and Lake Forest. Most, but not all, are affluent.

C&NW raised their fares during the 1893 depression, which infuriated many along the North Shore. Meanwhile, a new high-tech form of transportation, the electric streetcar, was a national sensation.

A group of North Shore financial backers decided the time was right to create a new railroad that would give the C&NW real competition, offering lower fares and more frequent service using electric streetcars that did not produce clouds of thick black smoke.

Thus, on June 25, 1894, the Bluff City Electric Street Railway was born. Its original goal was to run service between Waukegan and Lake Bluff. Service began on April 17, 1895.

To connect all the villages, towns, and cities along the North Shore took some doing, negotiating with every municipality along the way. Some demanded large cash payments, an elaborate station, or speed restrictions.

Streetcar lines connecting cities came to be known as "interurbans." They were forced to compete with existing steam railroads out of necessity to serve the same cities and towns that those steam railroads served. The new railroad built its line next to the Chicago & North Western.

Bankruptcies and corporate reorganizations were rife among early streetcar and interurban companies. The Bluff City Electric Street Railway became the Chicago & Milwaukee Electric Railway Company (C&ME) on May 12, 1898.

Service reached Highland Park on the north by June 23, 1898, and Evanston to the south the following year. At Church Street in Evanston, riders could travel to Chicago via the Chicago, Milwaukee, St. Paul & Pacific steam railroad (also known as the Milwaukee Road).

The Chicago & Milwaukee had ambitions to reach both cities, but it took some time to get there. Its tracks were shoehorned in next to the C&NW and ran on city streets in many town centers, which slowed down travel. The steam railroad refused to let its upstart competitor cross its tracks at grade level, so tunnels were built underneath it.

The C&ME built a branch line west to Libertyville in 1902, as a nearby quarry had the rock ballast needed for line extensions. This was extended farther west to the area now known as Mundelein in 1905.

During this period, A.C. Frost (1847–1924) led the railroad. Frost was a real estate speculator who hoped to make large profits developing areas where new lines were extended. Frost also owned the construction company that built new C&ME trackage and took payments in railroad stock.

In 1904, the interurban opened Ravinia Park on a 36-acre property in Highland Park, offering concerts that increased ridership on Sundays, otherwise a slow day. Ravinia remains a cultural icon of the North Shore, and millions have attended its concerts.

C&ME finally reached the Wisconsin state line in December 1905. It would take nearly three more years before service reached Milwaukee. The financial panic of 1907, brought on by risky banking practices, created widespread economic disruptions that quickly plunged the C&ME into bankruptcy and ousted A.C. Frost.

The interurban remained in receivership, under court supervision, until 1916. Although the railroad later referred to these as years of "stagnation," important improvements were made.

On May 16, 1908, the Northwestern Elevated Railroad took over the Milwaukee Road's commuter service north of Wilson Avenue in Chicago. This "Evanston Extension" connected with the C&ME at Church Street, as the Milwaukee Road had. The new electric service also created the possibility that C&ME interurban trains might one day go directly to downtown Chicago; although, this took more than a decade to become a reality.

After much wrangling, C&ME service finally reached downtown Milwaukee on October 31, 1908. The railroad also ran some local streetcar service in Milwaukee, as it already did in Waukegan.

Samuel Insull (1859–1938) became inventor Thomas Edison's personal secretary in 1881 and assumed greater and greater responsibilities for Edison's interests over the next two decades. Insull eventually set out on his own in Chicago, forming Commonwealth Edison in 1907. Insull's genius created the modern electrical grid, with widely distributed power, large power plants, and transmission lines, using economies of scale to offer more and more electricity at lower and lower rates. Streetcar and interurban companies were among his major customers and helped even out power consumption throughout the day. Insull began acquiring electric railroads, eventually owning all three major Chicago area interurbans and Chicago's "L" system. The C&ME reorganized into the Chicago North Shore & Milwaukee Railroad (CNS&M) on July 26, 1916, under Insull's control. It was branded as the North Shore Line (NSL).

Starting in 1915, NSL purchased new all-steel railcars, compatible with the clearances of the Chicago "L," but it still took a few years to negotiate trackage rights with the Milwaukee Road, which owned the "L" north of Wilson Avenue.

North Shore trains began operating directly to downtown Chicago on August 6, 1919, as far south as Roosevelt Road. This remained the primary destination until the end; although, a few trains ran to the south side from 1922 to 1938.

Rapid improvements were made under Insull management. Freight service was greatly expanded, including one of the very first piggyback trailer-on-flatcar operations. A less-than-carload "Merchandise Despatch" (Dispatch; Insull preferred the British spelling) service began. The fleet of wooden cars was gradually replaced by high-speed steel coaches. New stations were built, including a modern terminal in downtown Milwaukee. Dining car service began on March 31, 1917.

The North Shore Line offered high-speed service north of Waukegan, often up to 80 miles an hour, but trains were slowed through the congested North Shore suburbs. By 1923, the railroad had an answer—build a faster bypass route a few miles west of the existing Shore Line Route.

This new Skokie Valley Route, built at a cost of $10 million ($164 million in 2022 dollars) opened on June 5, 1926. An additional $10 million was spent on related improvements. Soon, the communities of Skokie, Glenview, Northfield, Northbrook, and Deerfield grew rapidly and became North Shore suburbs. Ridership continued to grow, as did profits.

Unfortunately, the Insull utility empire came crashing down in 1932, in the depths of the Great Depression. The North Shore Line went back into receivership and would not reemerge until 1946. Ridership plummeted. The railroad had an existential crisis in 1938 when the receiver ordered a 15-percent pay cut. The employees went on strike from August 16 to October 5, and no trains ran. Outright abandonment was considered, but modernization was chosen instead.

Besides modernizing existing coaches, two new streamlined, articulated high-speed "Electroliner" trains were ordered and went into service in early 1941. They were effective competition with the C&NW and Milwaukee Road's high-speed intercity trains.

A federal jobs program paid 45 percent of the cost of grade-separating nearly four miles of the Shore Line Route (and C&NW) through Winnetka between 1938 and 1943, an early example of government-funded transit improvements.

Ridership increased to new highs during World War II, in part due to gasoline and tire rationing and troop movements to and from Fort Sheridan and the Glenview Naval Air Station. Profits soared, but 1946 was the railroad's last profitable year.

Ridership declined in the postwar era, as the public clamored for autos and new highways to drive them on. The Edens expressway opened in 1951 and siphoned off ridership. Once the Northwest (now Kennedy) expressway opened in Chicago in 1960, highways paralleled practically the entire North Shore Line route to Milwaukee.

The railroad created a holding company, the Susquehanna Corporation, in 1953 to facilitate diversification and eventual abandonment of the railroad, as there were millions in tax advantages to be had. The Shore Line Route was abandoned on July 25, 1955.

In 1958, the railroad petitioned for final abandonment. No "white knight" came forward to save the line, and the Supreme Court rejected last-ditch efforts to forestall its demise.

Once the last North Shore Line trains arrived at their terminals in Milwaukee and Chicago, shortly after midnight on a very cold January 21, 1963, it truly was the "end of the line." After the last riders disembarked, the long process of dismantling this storied railroad began.

Author and historian William D. Middleton called it the end of the "interurban era" in the United States—not because the North Shore Line was the last one left (the South Shore Line continues), but it had been the shining example, America's fastest, a "super interurban."

When service ended, many considered the North Shore Line a failure, as it was losing money. The entire future of passenger train travel and public transit was in doubt. Some thought that trains had been replaced by a superior form of transit—the automobile.

In short, it was impossible for the North Shore Line to survive in the prevailing conditions of the time. There were fixed costs in offering frequent, convenient service, and revenues no longer covered those costs—with little chance the situation could be reversed.

The owners of this and many other passenger railroads were faced with a stark choice: either sell out to a government agency or liquidate the assets before they were dissipated. In 1963, there was no financial mechanism in place to save the North Shore Line.

By 1963, the North Shore Line's equipment had an average age of 38 years, which is quite a long time for railcars. The fleet was beginning to show its age, and its oldest cars were already 48 years old. Even the Electroliners were 22 years old. If service had continued, the entire fleet had to be replaced—and soon.

A valiant effort was made by the North Shore Commuters' Association (NSCA), led by Roy Roadcap (1920–1999), who hoped a coalition of riders and employees could purchase the railroad and restore it to profitability. While the NSCA was unsuccessful, it paved the way to later help save the South Shore Line and the rest of Chicago's commuter rail system.

Within a few short years of the North Shore Line's demise, and in part due to its loss, government help finally did arrive for the lucky survivors. The Philadelphia Suburban Transportation Company (also known as Red Arrow Lines), the last major privately owned electric transit operator in the nation, finally sold out to a public agency in 1970.

Faced with the imminent collapse of the nation's intercity passenger rail system, Congress created the National Railroad Passenger Corporation, now known as Amtrak, which took over the bulk of such services on May 1, 1971. Revenues are subsidized by a combination of state and federal funds. Now, transit agencies are thought to do well if half their monies come from the fare box.

The South Shore Line's owners declined to join Amtrak in 1971 and petitioned the Interstate Commerce Commission to abandon passenger service five years later, using many of the same arguments cited by the North Shore Line in their 1958 filing. As before, the public rallied to save the line, and this time, the outcome was different. The State of Indiana created the Northern Indiana Commuter Transportation District (NICTD) in 1977 to subsidize service.

Now, the South Shore Line is being expanded and upgraded. The Michigan City street running is being relocated onto private right-of-way, the single-track sections will be double-tracked, and a new branch line is under construction.

Faced with the impending collapse of much of Chicago's commuter rail system, voters in a six-county area approved creation of the Regional Transportation Authority (RTA) in 1974. It provides funding and oversight to various transit agencies, including Metra, created in 1982 to operate and contract out local commuter rail services.

If the North Shore Line had survived into the RTA era, chances are it would still be operating today, using new equipment, with the same kind of incremental improvements that are now being made on the South Shore Line. It would be permanent and indispensable.

The San Diego Trolley began service in 1981 and was an immediate success. This second-generation streetcar line soon expanded and, rechristened as "light rail," led to an electric transit renaissance in the United States, with dozens of new systems built. Now that roads and highways are clogged with autos across the nation, streetcars and interurbans, once considered obsolete, are desirable options for many cities.

Milwaukee opened a 2.1-mile initial modern streetcar line (branded as "The Hop") on November 2, 2018, returning electric trains to city streets 55 years after the North Shore Line's demise. While the North Shore Line will probably never be rebuilt, service has been restored elsewhere, on parts of other former interurbans.

The Chicago Transit Authority (CTA) began operating a five-mile segment of former North Shore Line trackage in April 1964 under a demonstration program partially funded by the federal government. The success of this "Skokie Swift," now the CTA Yellow Line, shows the North Shore Line had untapped potential for increasing ridership.

You can still experience part of the North Shore Line by riding the CTA Yellow Line and by riding any of the original cars that have been saved in museums and lovingly restored by volunteers.

Metra offers excellent commuter rail services to many suburbs once served by the North Shore Line, and Amtrak runs several daily trains between Chicago and Milwaukee.

The North Shore Line's employees were a close-kit bunch, who really considered themselves like a family, as did many of its riders. To become a North Shore Line fan today is to become a part of that family.

The North Shore Line is no longer considered obsolete. It was a pioneer of high-speed rail. It personified excellence, resourcefulness, and innovation. In the hearts and minds of its many fans, it will forever remain the "Road of Service."

This is its story.

—David Sadowski

CHICAGO NORTH SHORE AND MILWAUKEE RAILWAY

Over time, the North Shore Line became many different things, as shown in this place mat used for dining service starting in 1948. From left to right, one sees an Electroliner, offering intercity and commuter service; local buses; and electric freight.

One

BEGINNINGS

Chicago & Milwaukee cars Nos. 10 and 1 are pictured in Waukegan. Car No. 1 was built by Brill in 1898 for use in Waukegan. It was rebuilt into a line car in 1903. This is the second car No. 10, built by Pullman in 1899 for interurban use. It was retired in 1916. (Frank H. Butler photograph; Rex Butler collection.)

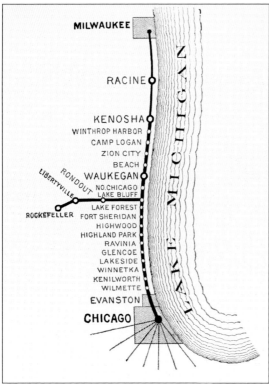

Frank H. Butler (1871–1963), at left, worked as a conductor and motorman for the Chicago & Milwaukee Electric from July 2, 1898, to March 11, 1899. On July 15, 1898, he paid $5 toward the cost of his uniform, leaving a balance of $15—$20 in 1898 is the equivalent of about $700 in 2022. Butler later worked as a photographer and owned a stationery store in Waukegan. Somehow, he managed to outlive the railroad, even though he had not worked there for more than 60 years. (Rex Butler collection.)

This 1908 map shows the extent of the Chicago & Milwaukee Electric Railroad's lines after service was finally extended to Milwaukee. Connections in Evanston were now made with the Northwestern Elevated Railroad instead of the Milwaukee Road.

The Chicago & Milwaukee Electric had no choice but to build tracks parallel to the existing Chicago & North Western steam railroad, as towns and cities had already grown up along its path. The Winnetka station, shown here, was replaced in the late 1930s, when both railroads were relocated by a grade separation project. The interurban's tracks were off to the right in this photograph, out of view.

This view is looking north along the Chicago & Milwaukee Electric right-of-way in downtown Wilmette in the early 1900s. Service was extended here in 1899, and the C&ME ran parallel to the Chicago & North Western tracks (located off to the left) from here to North Chicago.

This photograph shows the old Central Street Terminal in Evanston. At the station, one can just make out a Chicago & Milwaukee Electric wooden interurban car. Before 1919, this was where riders had to change trains for the rest of the trip into Chicago. The Northwestern Elevated Railroad took over service from the Milwaukee Road in 1908. This yard was closed after "L" service was extended north to Linden Avenue in Wilmette in 1912, which helps date the picture.

The Republic Construction Company was owned by A.C. Frost, head of the Chicago & Milwaukee Electric, and built much of the North Shore Line up until 1908. (Frank H. Butler photograph; Rex Butler collection.)

This real-photo postcard, dated August 1906, shows horse-drawn wagons grading the Chicago & Milwaukee Electric right-of-way as it was being extended north of Racine, Wisconsin. Horlicksville Road was located about two miles north of Racine, near where James and William Horlick had a factory that produced Horlicks malted milk.

In 1906, a Chicago Railways Company employee outing stops at the Libertyville station on the Chicago & Milwaukee Electric. This may be car No. 25, built by the Jewett Car Company in 1904. It was scrapped in 1930. (*Chicago Daily News* collection, DN-0006822, Chicago History Museum.)

C. M. STATION, LIBERTYVILLE ILL.

Taken from a real-photo postcard postmarked 1906, this image depicts the Chicago & Milwaukee Electric station in Libertyville. Passenger service was extended here in 1903, and the large station also served as a residence. It remained in use until the 1963 abandonment but has been demolished. One is looking east. Wooden car No. 10, the second to bear that number, was built by Pullman in 1899 and went out of service in 1916.

The C&ME extended service from Libertyville to what is now Mundelein on March 25, 1905, and this photograph was taken soon after. Compared to the one built in 1926, the original station was very spartan. This portion of the line was originally single-tracked, and a second track was later added, as well as an interchange connection with the Wisconsin Central, whose tracks were just west of here. The area had different names over the years—Rockefeller, when service commenced, and then the rather generic designation of "Area" before it was named for George Cardinal Mundelein (1872–1939) in 1925. (*Chicago Daily News* collection, DN-0006801, Chicago History Museum.)

While service on the C&ME's branch line to Libertyville began on July 15, 1902, the tracks were isolated from the rest of the line, as the Chicago & North Western refused to permit a crossing at grade. An underpass was built in Lake Bluff in 1904. This c. 1906 picture was taken on a Chicago Railways Company excursion. The Libertyville-Mundelein branch operated as a shuttle until 1926, when the Skokie Valley Route opened west of here, after which some trains went into Chicago. Shuttle service continued even after the Shore Line Route quit in 1955. (*Chicago Daily News* collection, DN-0006821, Chicago History Museum.)

In 1907, the Chicago & Milwaukee Electric built a large and attractive station in Lake Forest, just south of the Chicago & North Western's. This was probably done at the insistence of the city. It was not put into use until 1910, due to a mechanic's lien. Unfortunately, it was torn down around 1970.

Wood car No. 118 is stopped at Ravinia Park, sometime between 1915 and 1918. The man at right is Ellis Katz, with an unidentified man to his left, followed by his eventual wife, Agnes, who he married in 1917. A toboggan slide is visible to the right of the Chicago & North Western's tracks. Car No. 118 was built by the Jewett Car Company in 1906 and was retired in 1927. (J.J. Sedelmaier collection.)

A group of people walks toward the entrance to Ravinia Park in 1907, crossing the Chicago & Milwaukee Electric tracks. (Ravinia Park Collection, Highland Park Archives and Local History Collections.)

Here is the original North Shore Line station in Kenosha, Wisconsin, from an old postcard. It was replaced by one designed by Arthur U. Gerber, which opened on August 12, 1922. Wood car No. 133 was built by the Jewett Car Company in 1907 and rebuilt in 1914. The Chicago Aurora & Elgin purchased it in 1946 along with several other wood cars, which were all scrapped by 1954. (Douglas Davidson collection.)

Around 11:30 p.m. on April 22, 1908, the belt that turned a flywheel at the North Shore Electric power house in Waukegan caught fire, and it spread to the other equipment. While firemen were trying to put it out, there was an explosion, and the flywheel went through a wall, causing massive destruction. Two people were killed, and many more were injured. All of Waukegan lost power as a result. The North Shore Electric was a Samuel Insull utility, but Insull did not take control of the Chicago & Milwaukee Electric interurban until 1916, at which time it became the Chicago North Shore & Milwaukee, also known as the North Shore Line. Streetcars and interurbans were major customers of electric utilities and helped bring electric power to many rural areas. (Frank H. Butler photograph; Rex Butler collection.)

No. 402 was built by the Jewett Car Company in 1909 as a parlor-buffet car. It was converted to a coach in 1917 and retired in 1935. The following year, it was renumbered to No. 142 and leased to the Chicago Aurora & Elgin. After the war, it briefly returned to the NSL and was then sold to the CA&E in 1946. After CA&E cut back service to Forest Park in 1953, it was no longer needed and was scrapped.

When Samuel Insull descended the stairs of this railroad car on May 8, 1934, he was returning to Chicago to face trial over the collapse of his Midwest utilities empire. Since he was an honest businessman who continually tried to improve his companies, Insull was eventually acquitted of all charges, as was his son Samuel Jr.. The improvements he made in the North Shore Line allowed the railroad to outlast nearly all the other interurbans in the country.

This appeared on the cover of the December 1921 *North Shore Bulletin*, a magazine for riders. It encapsulates the Insull management's point of view, where the railroad's success was equally dependent on the owners, riders, and employees. It assumes the superiority of private enterprise, but many important improvements were made while the company was in receivership. Over time, the interests of ownership diverged from the public interest, as there was no longer a way to make a profit off the railroad.

The interior of an early North Shore Line diner is pictured above. Dining car service was offered from March 31, 1917, until 1947. After dining car service ended, No. 415 was the only one retained; it was used on charters and on the "Substitute Liner," which was used when one of the two Electroliners was in the shop for regularly scheduled maintenance.

Robert Heinlein captured this image of North Shore Line No. 772 on the Shore Line Route on June 9, 1955, about a month before the end of passenger service there. The exact location is not known, although it could be in Kenilworth. Although the interurban worked hard over the years to minimize the amount of street running, there where still stretches of it all the way up until the end. In some cases, the tracks were relocated onto private right-of-way. In a few instances, the tracks remained where they were, and the street itself was moved. In a few places, like here, there was nothing that could be done.

Within a few years of opening the new Milwaukee Terminal, two large neon signs were installed and were very effective advertising. One such sign went to the Illinois Railway Museum when the station was demolished in 1964.

The North Shore Line opened an attractive new station in Kenosha in 1922, designed by Insull staff architect Arthur U. Gerber. It served as the model for similar stations built a few years later in Niles Center (now Skokie) and Mundelein. Here, company officials pose in Kenosha while riding on the railroad's new observation car, No. 410, in 1923. (North Shore Line photograph; Robert Heinlein collection.)

Here is a c. 1923 view of rear observation car No. 410, posed with an Eastern Limited drumhead and company employees at the North Shore's headquarters in Highwood, Illinois. The interurban had several "named" trains in the 1920s for prestige value in competing for intercity traffic against the more established steam railroads. (North Shore Line photograph; Bruce Meyer collection, 2018.008.CNSM.Z.031, Lake States Railway Historical Association, Baraboo, Wisconsin.)

In 1923, the North Shore Line purchased four observation car trailers, Nos. 410 to 413. By 1932, they were taken out of service. Ridership reached an all-time high during World War II, so they were rebuilt as motorized coaches, with the ends enclosed, around 1942 or 1943. Of the four, only No. 411 survives, owned by the Escanaba & Lake Superior Railroad, whose headquarters are in Michigan. It is rarely seen. (J.J. Sedelmaier collection.)

Parlor/observation car No. 410 had plush armchairs like those found on main line railroads. The globe lights here harmonize well with those found in the new North Shore Line stations built in the 1920s, which were designed by Arthur U. Gerber. (North Shore Line photograph; Robert Heinlein collection.)

This special North Shore Line train is prepared to escort the famous Blue Devils of France to the Great Lakes Naval Training Station on May 26, 1919. The Blue Devils (Chasseurs Alpins) are an elite mountain infantry force of the French Army, established in 1888, and gained fame for their exploits during World War I. They made a very positive impact on the American public, and Irving Berlin wrote a song about them in 1918. North Shore trains did not go into regular service on the "L" until August 6, 1919, but occasionally ran there as early as 1917. While both companies were controlled by Insull, an arrangement had to be negotiated with the Milwaukee Road, which owned everything north of Wilson Avenue. Car No. 154, built by Brill in 1915, survived the abandonment but later fell victim to years of neglect and has been scrapped. (The National Archives.)

The North Shore Line began running into Chicago via the "L" in 1919. As more and more all-steel cars entered service, the wood ones were gradually phased out. Car No. 130 is at Roosevelt Road, most likely between 1926 and 1930, as it is signed for the Shore Line Route.

David A. Myers Jr. owns the original artwork used for four 1920s North Shore Line posters, including this one. He purchased them from the railroad after abandonment. The theme of this one, contrasting old and new forms of transportation, seems to relate directly to the exhibit shown in the next picture.

North Shore Line car No. 731 and train are pictured at the Wisconsin State Fair in 1927. Access to the fairgrounds was via Milwaukee Electric trackage. People throng to examine the new North Shore all-steel coaches. How fast could they go? They were excellent performers, and their balancing speed (when maximum tractive effort equals the resistance) when trained was 85 miles per hour. Eighty miles per hour was routine, and the railroad promoted this extensively in its 1920s advertising.

A new Milwaukee Terminal opened on September 15, 1920, at Sixth Street and Sycamore Street (later changed to Michigan Street). The portion at left housed the North Shore Restaurant from 1920 to 1927, but it was not yet ready when the station was dedicated. (J.J. Sedelmaier collection.)

Here is the interior of the Milwaukee Terminal when it was new. The lunch counter remained until 1963, but the ticket booth was eventually expanded. In later years, there was a photo booth where one could take his or her own picture. (J.J. Sedelmaier collection.)

The North Shore Restaurant occupied the northeast corner of the terminal from 1920 to 1927, but it did not develop enough business and was closed. A variety of other tenants occupied the space over the years. (J.J. Sedelmaier collection.)

Construction of the Skokie Valley Route was underway on January 23, 1925, in this view looking northwest from the Howard Street "L" station. The section to Dempster in Niles Center (now Skokie) was completed first so the Chicago Rapid Transit Company could begin local service. Then construction began north of Dempster. (North Shore Line photograph; Bruce Meyer collection, 2018.008.CNSM.Z.030, Lake States Railway Historical Association, Baraboo, Wisconsin.)

On May 19, 1926, just two weeks prior to the opening of the Skokie Valley Route, the "Insull Spanish" Sheridan Elms station in west Lake Forest is under construction. It was a wood frame building with a stucco covering and a tile roof. It no longer exists, but the very similar Briergate station survives. Skokie Highway 41 would run just a hundred feet or so to the east of here after 1935. (Harold G. Mason photograph for the North Shore Line, History Center of Lake Forest-Lake Bluff collection, 2002.37.35.)

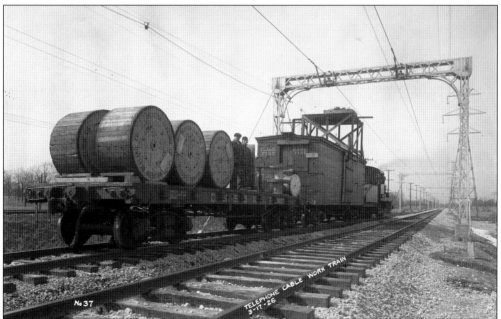

On March 17, 1926, a North Shore work train strings telephone cables north of Niles Center Road on the as yet unfinished Skokie Valley Route. (North Shore Line photograph; Bruce Meyer collection, 2018.008.CNSM.Z.034, Lake States Railway Historical Association, Baraboo, Wisconsin.)

Coach No. 755 is at the Milwaukee Terminal in August 1959. The terminal opened in 1920, taking advantage of the natural slope of the terrain. Riders entered at street level on the north end of the station and came out the south end at platform level for easy boarding of trains. Prior to 1920, interurban trains loaded and unloaded right in the street at Second Street and Wisconsin Avenue, a few blocks from here. These were the types of improvements that set the Insull properties far ahead of their competitors. (Jeffrey L. Wien photograph.)

The 28th Eucharistic Congress, held June 20–24, 1926, in the Chicago Archdiocese, was a huge event that the North Shore Line played a major part in. On closing day of the congress, nearly one million people attended an outdoor Mass in Mundelein. The interurban helped transport between 200,000–300,000 people that day. A year of planning was involved. Even more remarkable, success largely depended on the new Skokie Valley Route, which had only opened on June 5. The picture shows the *Cardinal's Special*, which escorted many dignitaries to Mundelein. (J.J. Sedelmaier collection.)

Two

THE MILWAUKEE DIVISION

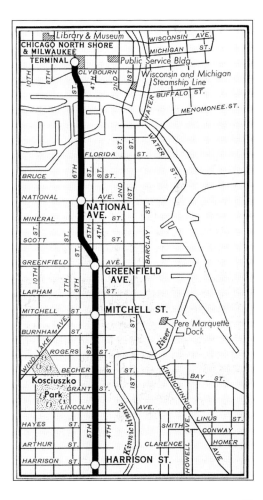

Milwaukee was already a major city by the time the Chicago & Milwaukee Electric (C&ME) extended service there in 1908, entering the city over 2.8 miles of city streets. Various plans were put forth over the years to relocate the tracks onto private right-of-way, but the street running remained until the end. The railroad cited the potential cost of relocation onto an expressway median as a factor in its 1958 abandonment filing. C&ME also operated local streetcars on its tracks, which went some distance past the terminal, built in 1920.

Here is a May 4, 1958, view of the Milwaukee Terminal at Sixth and Michigan Streets, looking southeast. Part of the building (at left) was then occupied by the Greyhound Travel Bureau. In the 1920s, this was the location of the North Shore Restaurant. By the time the interurban quit, the railroad's commissary was there. (William C. Hoffman photograph.)

The waiting room interior at the Milwaukee Terminal is pictured in 1963. (Ed Wilkommen photograph/collection, 2018.15.SM.247-11, Lake States Railway Historical Association, Baraboo, Wisconsin.)

Here is the platform entrance at the Milwaukee Terminal as it appeared in January 1963. The ground slopes in this area, so one could enter the building at the north end at street level, walk through, and come out at the high-level train platforms on the other side. (Ed Wilkommen photograph/ collection, 2018.15.SM.247-09, Lake States Railway Historical Association, Baraboo, Wisconsin.)

Silverliner No. 756 is at the Milwaukee Terminal on June 22, 1962. The platforms here were very similar to those on the Chicago "L." (Nick Jenkins photograph.)

The low angle here creates a dramatic image of an Electroliner at the Milwaukee Terminal in 1960. How fast did they go? A fully loaded Electroliner had a balancing speed of 78 miles per hour but routinely went 85–90 miles per hour in service. In a 1950 test run, with field shunts added, one was clocked at 111 miles per hour. These were removed, as speeds this fast did not allow crossing gates enough time to close. It also would have put too much strain on the motors. (John V. Engleman photograph.)

A Silverliner pulls out onto Sixth Street from the Milwaukee Terminal, most likely in the late 1950s.

North Shore Line Electroliner Nos. 801–802 has just left the Milwaukee Terminal at Sixth Street and Clybourn Avenue on October 31, 1948. (Richard H. Young photograph.)

Car No. 741 creeps south along the old Sixth Street viaduct in Milwaukee, next to a 1958 Chevy. Due to the vibrations a faster speed would create, train speed on part of the bridge was limited to four miles per hour. No. 741 was built by Pullman in 1928 and modernized in 1940.

An Electroliner passes fantrip coach No. 175 between Fifth and Sixth Streets in Milwaukee on April 19, 1959. A few years after track abandonment, this area became a short street that serves as an access road for a nearby expressway. (Raymond DeGroote Jr. photograph.)

A northbound Electroliner is on Fifth Street at Maple Street in Milwaukee, approaching St. Stanislaus Church. The buildings on the right side of this early-1950s view have been replaced by the Interstate 94 expressway.

Electroliner No. 803–804 is northbound on Fifth Street at Maple Street in Milwaukee on January 13, 1963. All the buildings on the right have been demolished and replaced by an expressway. (Jeffrey L. Wien photograph.)

North Shore Line coach No. 759 heads up a two-car train heading southbound on Fifth Street at Harrison Avenue, leaving street running in favor of private right-of-way in Milwaukee on June 16, 1962. (Richard H. Young photograph.)

Here is a northbound Electroliner on an embankment at Sixth Street and Oklahoma Avenue in Milwaukee in 1962. This view is looking west. North of here, the ground slopes upward and brought the tracks to ground level, where trains continued north on city streets, starting at Harrison Avenue. (W.N. Higginbotham photograph.)

A northbound three-car "Substitute Liner" crosses the Milwaukee Road in Milwaukee, Wisconsin, on January 4, 1963. When one of the two Electroliners went into the shop for regularly scheduled maintenance, a substitute train went in its place, using unpowered dining car No. 415 in the middle. This bridge, as well as its approaches, was the only single-track section on the North Shore Line, other than the Glencoe gauntlet on the Shore Line Route. (Marty Bernard photograph.)

Here is an Electroliner at Grange Avenue, in the south part of Milwaukee. This is just west of General Mitchell International Airport. (W.N. Higginbotham photograph.)

In January 1963, southbound Electroliner passes the Ryan interlocking tower, where the interurban crossed the Chicago & North Western New Line at an angle in Milwaukee County. (Lee Hastman photograph/collection, 2010.030.C.03.045, Lake States Railway Historical Association, Baraboo, Wisconsin.)

Cars Nos. 756 and 772 meet at Racine, Wisconsin, in November 1962. Note the nearby Piggly Wiggly supermarket, a Wisconsin institution. For some reason, this station was never modernized, unlike Kenosha. (Ed Wilkommen photograph/collection, 2018.15.SM.245-15, Lake States Railway Historical Association, Baraboo, Wisconsin.)

The railroad had power positioned at strategic points along the right-of-way. This Mercury arc substation was at Four Mile Road north of Racine, and this is how it looked on June 17, 1962. This building still stands, having been purchased by a local farmer after its abandonment for use as a stable. (Robert Heinlein photograph.)

A two-car train of Silverliners approaches the Ryan interlocking tower in the vicinity of Racine, Wisconsin, on January 13, 1963. The North Shore Line crossed the Chicago & North Western's New Line tracks here at grade. (Jeffrey L. Wien photograph.)

Here is the North Shore Line's massive Zion station, as it looked in the early 1960s. The elders in what started out as a religious community insisted that the railroad build a station this size, anticipating rapid growth that did not materialize. The station was torn down within a few years of the interurban's 1963 abandonment. Zion's current population is about 23,500.

The Milwaukee Electric interurban had several lines radiating from Milwaukee, including service to Racine and Kenosha (the M-R-K line), competition for the North Shore Line. This line was abandoned by the end of 1947. On December 4, 1949, Milwaukee Electric car No. 1121 was allowed to run on a railfan trip on the North Shore Line. Here, it is heading south at the Kenosha station. No. 1121 was built by the Kuhlman Car Company in 1909. The single-ended car went as far as Green Bay Junction near Rondout, where it could be turned via a wye. After the Chicago Aurora & Elgin was abandoned, there was a plan to operate one of its cars on a North Shore railfan trip, but the railroad would not permit it.

Not all the railroad's crossings were protected by gates. This is the Five Mile Road crossing, north of Racine, Wisconsin, like many others along sparsely populated areas of the line. Richard H. Young took this picture on June 12, 1962.

Three

THE SHORE LINE ROUTE

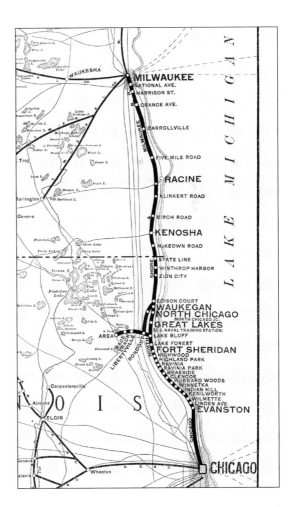

This map, taken from the 1917 annual report, shows the extent of the railroad once it reached Milwaukee in 1908. High-speed operation was possible north of Waukegan, but intercity service was much slower in the North Shore suburbs. That problem was solved when a new bypass, the Skokie Valley Route, was built a few miles to the west of the existing alignment, which then became known as the Shore Line Route. This map was made two years before NSL trains were able to operate on the "L" south of Evanston. What is now known as Mundelein was called "Area" from 1909 to 1925.

On March 25, 1962, a Central Electric Railfans' Association railfan trip used North Shore Line cars Nos. 771, 415, 753, and 251 on the CTA Evanston branch, where NSL cars had last run in 1955, when the Shore Line Route was abandoned. Here, the train is at Isabella. This lightly used station closed in 1973 and was removed soon after. (William C. Hoffman photograph.)

On July 17, 1955, a Shore Line Route train turns south onto private right-of-way from Greenleaf Avenue in Wilmette. After making a station stop, it will continue south into Chicago via CTA trackage starting at Linden Avenue. The interurbans were restricted to 15 miles per hour (and eight miles per hour at intersections) by local ordinance and could not run express. If anyone was waiting for a train, it had to stop and pick them up. (Joseph Canfield photograph; David Stanley collection.)

One is looking west along Greenleaf Avenue on October 24, 1948, just west of Eighth Street. A westbound two-car train, with No. 178 at the rear, passes by, while the lady at left appears to be waiting for an eastbound train due to arrive. Car No. 178 was built by Cincinnati Car Company in September 1920. After the arrival of newer coaches, it and other similar cars were relegated to the Shore Line and Mundelein branches.

This view is looking northeast on Greenleaf Avenue from a second-floor bedroom window at 531 Eighth Street in December 1950. The photographer lived at 711 Eighth Street, a few blocks away, but apparently was friends with a couple who lived at this address, which had an excellent vantage point for pictures of the street running operation. (William E. Robertson photograph; Eric Bronsky collection.)

One sees the same bedroom window view on June 18, 1955, a month before the end of service on Greenleaf Avenue. A woman has just gotten off a Shore Line train that includes car No. 412, built by the Cincinnati Car Company in 1924. It was originally a trailer observation car, and these were out of service in 1932. No. 412 was converted into a two-motor coach in 1943. (William E. Robertson photograph; Eric Bronsky collection.)

Car No. 168 heads up a three-car Chicago Local on the Shore Line Route, stopping at Linden Avenue in Wilmette. The date is February 11, 1939, and this view is looking north. North of this station, the line curved to the west and went onto Greenleaf Avenue. The building at left still exists, with a second story added.

Car No. 163 heads up a southbound two-car train at the Wilmette station (East Railroad and Greenleaf Avenues) on October 24, 1948. The train is about to turn east onto Greenleaf Avenue for one mile, after which it will head south and join up with the Chicago Transit Authority's Evanston "L" branch. No. 163 was built by Brill in 1915. (Richard H. Young photograph.)

Wood car No. 305 is on the street in Kenilworth in 1929. It was built by the American Car Company in 1910. In 1936, it was converted to a sleet cutter (to keep ice off the overhead wires in the winter) and was scrapped in 1940.

Central Electric Railfans' Association held a farewell fantrip on the Shore Line Route on July 24, 1955, the day prior to the abandonment. The train, made up of coaches Nos. 155, 187, and 154, posed for pictures by the historic municipal fountain in Kenilworth, designed by noted Prairie School architect George W. Maher (1864–1926). The fountain, built in 1900, was paid for by the Chicago & Milwaukee Electric as part of the tribute the interurban made in exchange for being allowed to operate through the village. It has since been renovated. (Raymond DeGroote Jr. photograph.)

A Shore Line Route train crosses Elm Street in Winnetka in 1930. These tracks were relocated into an open cut, approximately where the photographer was standing, as part of the 1938–1943 Winnetka Grade Separation Project. (Chicago History Museum, ICHi-098644; Charles R. Childs, photographer.)

As the Great Depression worsened in the early 1930s, ridership fell, and the North Shore Line had less and less use for its older wood coaches. Their last use was in school tripper service for New Trier High School around 1934, which this photograph may show. No. 134 was built by the Jewett Car Company in 1907 and rebuilt in 1914. It was leased to the Chicago Aurora & Elgin in 1936, which eventually purchased it. No. 134 was retired in 1948.

This December 31, 1929, view, looking east, is of the North Shore Line crossing at South Avenue in Glencoe on the Shore Line Route. The photographer was documenting Chicago & North Western facilities, with tracks adjacent to the North Shore Line. It is fortunate that he captured this view of a two-car wooden North Shore train. One can see how having two railroads running next to each other, with two sets of gates, created a dangerous situation. The Winnetka Grade Separation Project helped alleviate that problem. (Stanton Wilhite photograph; John S. Ingles collection, 2021.003.PCNW-08, Lake States Railway Historical Association, Baraboo, Wisconsin.)

The beginnings of the Winnetka Grade Separation Project at Elm Street are pictured in 1939. Work began in December 1938 and was not completed until 1943. The idea of relocating the tracks of the two railroads here had been gestating for more than 20 years, but other than design work, nothing much happened until two prominent citizens were killed in 1937 when they were hit by a Chicago & North Western freight train that was backing up at night without any lights on. Winnetka applied for federal funding as a jobs program in the Great Depression, and it was quickly approved. (Winnetka Historical Society collection.)

By June 16, 1940, when this picture was taken, the Winnetka Grade Separation Project was well underway. North Shore Line trains are operating in the new open cut but are temporarily using what will eventually become the Chicago & North Western tracks. They began doing this on November 28, 1939. The permanent tracks went into service in September 1940 and included an automatic block signaling system.

A southbound Shore Line train approaches Hubbard Woods station in Winnetka on June 27, 1954. The tracks and stations for both the North Shore Line and Chicago & North Western Railway were relocated from ground level into an open cut between 1938 and 1943 by the Winnetka Grade Separation Project. This Public Works Administration project originally called for a small North Shore station here, but the railroad wanted something bigger, which cost an additional $14,000. Car No. 168 was built by the Jewett Car Company in 1917. (William C. Hoffman photograph.)

While the Winnetka Grade Separation Project mostly put railroad tracks into an open cut, the southernmost portion was elevated onto an embankment instead. This was due in part to natural topography, but also in anticipation that eventually, the tracks in Wilmette and Kenilworth would be elevated, which has not happened. Here, photographer Raymond DeGroote Jr. captured coaches Nos. 175 and 413 (left) and No. 155 (right) at the Indian Hill stop in Winnetka on July 24, 1955.

On June 9, 1955, a northbound two-car Shore Line Route train has just come off a side street onto a wooded area next to the C&NW right-of-way. This may be in Kenilworth. (Robert Heinlein photograph.)

Over time, nearly all the Shore Line Route became double-tracked, excepting one short bridge in Glencoe that could not support the weight of two passing trains. Here, Silverliner 766 runs the gauntlet on an August 9, 1953, railfan trip. (William C. Hoffman photograph.)

Car No. 154 heads up a southbound railfan trip train at the entrance to Ravinia Park on July 24, 1955, shortly before the Shore Line was abandoned. (George Krambles photograph; Raymond DeGroote Jr. collection.)

World-famous architect Frank Lloyd Wright designed a modest shelter for the North Shore Line, built in 1917 at Maple Hill and Old Green Bay Road in Glencoe. It no longer exists, but there have been proposals to build a replica on the original site, which is now a trail. (J.J. Sedelmaier collection.)

The North Shore station at Ravinia (not to be confused with Ravinia Park), designed by Arthur U. Gerber and built in 1925, was an intriguing blend of Prairie style and Bungalow Vernacular architecture. It is a link between Gerber's station designs for the Niles Center "L" branch and the Kenosha, Dempster, and Mundelein terminals. (Douglas Davidson collection.)

This view is looking south from Central Avenue in Highland Park around 1930. The Shore Line Route tracks are at right. A small shelter is visible. The area the North Shore Line once occupied is now a parking lot.

This view is looking north along the Shore Line Route in Highland Park around 1930. NSL tracks ran parallel to the nearby Chicago & North Western Railway at left.

Silverliner No. 766 is stopped in Highland Park on August 9, 1953, by the Chicago & North Western station. NSL trains ran for a short distance in the street, as there was not sufficient room there for a private right-of-way. (Robert Selle photograph.)

The North Shore Line's headquarters in Highwood, built in 1905, served as the general office of the railroad until 1963. The porch area was enclosed to provide more office space. Line car No. 604 is out front.

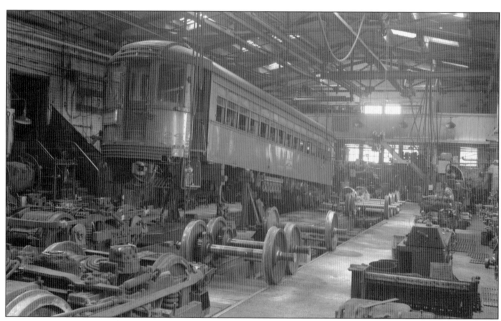

Car No. 724 is seen in an undated photograph at the Highwood Shops. Much of the credit for the railroad's exemplary work in maintaining its fleet is due to master mechanic Henry Cordell (1875–1971), still working there in 1963 in his late 80s. No. 724 was built by the Cincinnati Car Company in 1926 and modernized in 1939. (Ed Wilkommen photograph/collection, 2018.15. N99B.2873, Lake States Railway Historical Association, Baraboo, Wisconsin.)

Here is the newly modernized interior of a North Shore Line coach in 1940. Forty-eight such cars were upgraded between 1939 and 1941 at the Highwood Shops. (North Shore Line company photograph.)

A 700-series car is being repainted as a Silverliner at the Highwood Shops on July 13, 1955. The steel cars did not actually have fluted sides—they were painted to look as if they did, a trompe l'oeil (literally, a "trick of the eye"), a process which took a few days of careful painting to pull off. (Robert Selle photograph.)

This c. 1923 view of the North Shore Line's attractive Lake Forest station shows why a retaining wall was needed on the east side by McKinley Road, just south of Deerpath Road. The Chicago and North Western station (now Metra) is just north of here. (Harold G. Mason photograph for the North Shore Line, History Center of Lake Forest-Lake Bluff collection, 2002.39.2.)

NSL No. 186 is on the tail end of a railfan trip train at Deerpath Road in Lake Forest on December 28, 1962. Although this was more than seven years after the Shore Line abandonment, the railroad still had a single track in service for part of the old route, to access the Highwood Shops and for freight. The Chicago & North Western commuter station is at left. (Jeffrey L. Wien photograph.)

Car No. 172 is northbound at Fort Sheridan on July 4, 1955. Note the substation at left. (Raymond DeGroote Jr. photograph.)

Cars Nos. 155 and 168 meet at Fourteenth Street in North Chicago on July 24, 1955. Abbott Labs is at right. No. 155, at left, is southbound on a Central Electric Railfans' Association railfan trip just prior to the Shore Line abandonment. (Raymond DeGroote Jr. photograph.)

Both the Shore Line and Skokie Valley Routes served the North Chicago Junction station, as did Waukegan city streetcars, making this an important transfer point. On July 4, 1955, car No. 772 is running southbound on the Shore Line. It was built by the Standard Steel Car Company in 1930 and modernized in 1950, although not as a Silverliner. (William C. Hoffman photograph.)

This was scanned from an original North Shore Line eight-by-ten-inch nitrate negative, taken around 1930, in the collections of Robert Heinlein. The car is No. 714, signed as a Chicago Local on the Shore Line Route. The location is between Sixteenth and Seventeenth Streets in North Chicago, looking north. The freight siding at left served the Thomas J. Killian Plumbing Supply Company. Freight trains had to stop before passing the high-level platform seen here, so that the outer part could be flipped up for clearances. The Chicago & North Western's tracks were a short distance east of here, to the right out of view of this photograph.

North Shore Line car No. 182 heads south in North Chicago, Illinois, on June 12, 1954. No. 182 was built by the Cincinnati Car Company in 1920. In the distance, at left, one can see a Chicago & North Western train made up of Budd Rail Diesel (RDC) cars, which were self-propelled coaches. The railroad used three such RDCs in commuter service for a short time, but the experiment was unsuccessful, and it turned instead to using bi-levels and diesel locomotives. C&NW RDC No. 9933 is now at the Illinois Railway Museum. (Robert Selle photograph.)

On July 9, 1955, car No. 708 heads up a southbound Shore Line train, having just left the Tenth Street station at the border between Waukegan and North Chicago. No. 708 was built by the Cincinnati Car Company in 1924. (Robert Selle photograph.)

Once the Skokie Valley Route opened on June 5, 1926, Shore Line trains no longer ran to Milwaukee but terminated here at the Court Street station in Waukegan. On June 16, 1940, wood car No. 300 (built by the Jewett Car Company in 1909) was on a Central Electric Railfans' Association railfan trip, while steel car No. 169 (built by Jewett in 1917) is in regular service. When buses replaced Waukegan's streetcars on November 16, 1947, the Shore Line Terminal was moved to the Tenth Street station on the border between Waukegan and North Chicago.

After the NSL abandoned streetcar service in Waukegan in 1947, Shore Line Route trains terminated at the outskirts of town, at Tenth Street. Steel coach No. 172 was built by the Cincinnati Car Company in September 1920. After spending several decades at the Indiana Transportation Museum, it went to the Illinois Railway Museum in 2018, where it will be restored.

On July 23, 1955, John D. Emery, then president of the Evanston Historical Society, purchased the last Shore Line ticket sold at the Church Street station from agent George Kennedy. The ticket window was closed the following day (Sunday), and the last Shore Line train ran in the early hours of July 25 (Monday). The ticket remains in the historical society collection. Emery was later mayor of Evanston (1962–1970), during which time he vetoed an antidiscrimination housing ordinance. (Dwight Furness photograph; Evanston Photographic Studios.)

One is looking south toward the CTA Linden Avenue yard in Wilmette on July 26, 1955. The rail connection between the North Shore Line and the CTA has been severed here, as the Shore Line Route has now been abandoned. (William E. Robertson photograph; Eric Bronsky collection.)

This is the view looking north along Poplar Drive at Greenleaf Avenue in downtown Wilmette on March 18, 1956, while the rails were being removed at what had once been the North Shore Line station. The interurban held off on this work for several months, while waiting to see if the Chicago Transit Authority wanted to purchase the Shore Line Route—which it did not. (William E. Robertson photograph; Eric Bronsky collection.)

Here is a view of the Shore Line Route at Elm Place in Highland Park on November 24, 1956, looking north by northwest. Everything south of here has been abandoned. That was the portion of the line that did not have freight service. (William E. Robertson photograph; Eric Bronsky collection.)

Four

THE SKOKIE VALLEY ROUTE

With the opening of the Skokie Valley Route in 1926, the North Shore Line reached the pinnacle of its success. Now, the old Shore Line Route served as a commuter line, while intercity passengers could take advantage of the new high-speed bypass route a few miles to the west. The areas around the new line developed rapidly, but it would still be many years before they had substantial population.

Electroliner Nos. 803–804 speed west through the Evanston cut on June 3, 1962, approaching Asbury Avenue. In the distance, one can see the former Niles Center "L" station at Ridge Avenue, designed by Arthur U. Gerber, in use from 1925 to 1948. (Raymond DeGroote Jr. photograph.)

One of the two Electroliners crosses the North Shore Channel on October 21, 1950. After the abandonment of the North Shore Line in 1963, this became part of the route of the CTA Skokie Swift, today's Yellow Line. This is near the border between Skokie and Evanston.

A northbound North Shore Line train stops at Dempster in January 1963, the final month. Just over a year later, after the abandonment, the CTA resumed service between here and Howard as the Skokie Swift. Note the sign at left for a yarn store in the terminal building.

Silverliner No. 763 is at speed near Green Bay Road in Lake Bluff on June 12, 1962. (Jeffrey L. Wien photograph.)

Here is the view looking west from Green Bay Road overpass on June 17, 1962, in Lake Bluff. The Skokie Valley Route is at right, with the Mundelein branch at left. This was the only place on the North Shore where four tracks were under catenary. Electroliner Nos. 803–804 approach, while a train, including car No. 251, heads away from view. (Robert Heinlein photograph.)

Seaboard Coast Line streamlined diesel train No. 4900 was built in 1936 by St. Louis Car Company and was an obvious influence on the design of the North Shore Line Electroliners, built by the same manufacturer in 1939–1941. No. 4900 was scrapped in 1971 after Amtrak took over intercity passenger rail service. It is shown here in August 1969 and was originally Seaboard Air Line No. 2028. Like the Electroliners, it was one of a pair.

Here is a classic view of a southbound Electroliner on the Skokie Valley Route, at speed under catenary wire, approaching the Lake Bluff station in October 1962. (Bruce Meyer photograph/ collection, 2018.008.CNSM.I.086, Lake States Railway Historical Association, Baraboo, Wisconsin.)

Moving trains posed quite a problem for photographers in an earlier era, as film speeds were quite slow by today's standards. If one waited until the train was close, the results would often have motion blur. By trial and error, some photographers developed a technique called "panning," moving the camera while the exposure was made. This is an excellent example by Nick Jenkins, taken on April 16, 1961, and really conveys a sense of motion.

Here are two tickets, both used on June 19, 1962, and punched by a conductor. Each conductor had a different shaped punch so their work could be identified later if needed.

The North Shore Line's Woodridge station is seen in August 1962. This was one of several 1920s-era stations designed in "Insull Spanish." They were wooden-frame buildings covered with stucco and had tile roofs. The Woodridge station was demolished after the North Shore Line shut down in 1963.

Silverliner No. 759 and "Greenliner" No. 160 pose side-by-side at Edison Court in Waukegan on January 12, 1963. Unlike Silverliner, the name Greenliner was an unofficial one; although, it was in use as early as 1938. No. 160 was on the final railfan trip, sponsored by Central Electric Railfans' Association. (William C. Hoffman photograph.)

Here is an Electroliner at Edison Court in Waukegan on May 26, 1959. Edison Court was an important station, as cars were added and cut there. Less service was needed north of Waukegan, so cars were often cut when heading north and added when heading south. One can see where cars were stored on a siding next to the main line. This is a prime example of a "three-quarter view" of a railcar, prized by many railfan photographers.

Conductor Bruce Carlson raises the trolley pole "on the fly" near East Prairie Road on July 8, 1961. This was the changeover point from third rail to overhead wire, and the transition was made while the train was moving. This required both skill and daring. When the CTA resumed service here in 1964, this changeover was motorized and controlled by the operator, as there was no conductor. Carlson's employment started on May 25, 1961, and by the end of service, he had become a motorman. (John Gruber photograph 03-028-081, Collection of the Center for Railroad Photography & Art.)

Here is a view of Oakton Street in Skokie, looking west, on December 11, 1931. The tracks with overhead wire were used by the North Shore Line and the Chicago Rapid Transit Company's Niles Center branch. Both were running on the NSL's Skokie Valley Route, and this portion was built in 1925. The other set of tracks belong to the Chicago & North Western and were used for freight.

On September 4, 1961, Raymond DeGroote Jr. took this photograph of a four-car train (Nos. 409, 750, 764, and 156) as it headed southbound on the Skokie Valley Route at Green Bay Junction. Here, the line crossed the Mundelein branch, where a fantrip train is visible off in the distance. Many of the riders had gotten off the train for this photo opportunity, made more dramatic by smoking brakes.

An Electroliner is "at speed" at Green Bay Road on a snowy January 19, 1963. (Raymond DeGroote Jr. photograph.)

The control cab of Electroliner No. 802, seen here on May 20, 1962, included an admonition against spitting. (William C. Hoffman photograph.)

Here is a January 1963 view inside the tavern/lounge car in one of the Electroliners. (Ed Wilkommen photograph/collection, 2018.15.SM.252-006, Lake States Railway Historical Association, Baraboo, Wisconsin.)

Celebrities like Bob Hope (1903–2003), star of stage, screen, radio, and television, were often photographed while traveling by train between Chicago and Milwaukee. This was very effective advertising for the North Shore Line, and it also promoted Hope's latest film, *The Lemon Drop Kid*, released on March 8, 1951. It was based on a short story with the same name by Damon Runyan (1880–1946) and also starred Marilyn Maxwell (1921–1972). The song "Silver Bells" was introduced in this film. This advertisement appeared in local newspapers in southern Wisconsin. (Courtesy of Ed Oslowski.)

Here is the interior of an Electroliner tavern/lounge car as it ran on the streets of Milwaukee on June 17, 1962. (William C. Hoffman photograph.)

When the Electroliners were introduced in 1941, the North Shore Line still offered fine dining service on some of its other trains. They were already serving beef tenderloin but needed something informal for the Liners, as they ran throughout the day and not just at meal times. The famous Electroburger was actually steak mixed with beef fat, salt and pepper, egg, and Worcestershire sauce—a high-class pub burger. For $1.40 in 1962 (equal to $13.40 in 2022), one received "Selected beef-tenderloin cooked to retain all its juicy delicious flavor, served on a tasty roll, with potato chips, relish, and coffee, tea, or milk," as the menu put it. Here is an Electroburger from May 9, 1962, served with an upside-down can of Pabst Blue Ribbon beer (before pop tops were introduced). This was not an inexpensive meal; at the time, a White Castle burger cost 12¢. (William C. Hoffman photograph.)

This view shows the coupling and diaphragm between Silverliners No. 415 (dining car) and No. 768 (coach) on a special excursion train in Northbrook during February 1960. The diaphragm allowed passengers to go back and forth from the coach to the dining car. Riders on the Electroliners could do this because it was all one unit, with diaphragms built in. (Richard H. Young photograph.)

The interior of diner No. 415 is pictured in November 1962. After regular dining car service ended in 1947, No. 415 was the only one retained for use on charters and on the "Substitute Liner," when one of the Electroliners was in the shop. (Ed Wilkommen photograph/collection, 2018.15. SM.252-005, Lake States Railway Historical Association, Baraboo, Wisconsin.)

Sailors cross from one platform to another as both Electroliners meet at North Chicago Junction in May 1962. (Jim Martin photograph.)

A woman in high heels and wearing a long skirt negotiates the rails just after getting off an Electroliner at North Chicago Junction in the early 1950s.

Five

THE MUNDELEIN BRANCH

Steel coach No. 160, built by Brill in 1915, is at the east end of the Mundelein branch in Lake Bluff. The underpass connected the branch line with the Shore Line Route and the Highwood Shops. Farther west, the line crossed the Skokie Valley Route at grade. No. 160, now at the Illinois Railway Museum, is the second-oldest surviving car, after No. 162, which went into service first.

Car No. 718 crosses the Chicago & North Western's tracks in Lake Bluff, bound for Chicago. Much of the Mundelein branch ran parallel to Route 176 and has since been converted to a hiking and biking trail. (Jeffrey L. Wien photograph.)

Richard H. Young took this picture in Lake Bluff on June 2, 1960, from the back of a moving North Shore car. One is looking east toward South Upton tower, with Route 176 at left (north), having just crossed the Chicago & North Western's tracks. One of the line cars is on the eastbound track.

Electroliner Nos. 803–804 made an unusual appearance on the Mundelein branch on a February 17, 1957, railfan trip. Here, it is at Rondout, where an embankment took it over the Milwaukee Road. (Robert Heinlein photograph.)

NSL No. 715 crosses the DesPlaines River in Libertyville on June 16, 1962. This car was built by the Cincinnati Car Company in 1926. It was modernized in 1939. After the 1963 abandonment, it was first purchased by the Mid-Continent Railroad Museum. Since 1988, it has been at the Fox River Trolley Museum in South Elgin, Illinois. (Jeffrey L. Wien photograph.)

Here is the Libertyville station in January 1963, shortly before the end.

The North Shore Line had numerous freight sidings that often ran some distance from the main line. This picture, taken by William C. Hoffman on August 9, 1953, shows car No. 169 on a railfan trip, near the end of a spur line that served a lumberyard in Libertyville. This car was built by the Jewett Car Company in 1917.

The Perpetual Adoration stop on the Mundelein branch served a Catholic religious site in Libertyville that offered Eucharistic adoration 24 hours a day. Although not a major stop (it only had a small shelter), the name appealed to many fans of the North Shore Line, as it expressed their feelings for the railroad. Here, car No. 182, built in 1920 by the Cincinnati Car Company, heads east on June 16, 1962. (Jeffrey L. Wien photograph.)

Raymond DeGroote Jr. took this close-up picture of the Perpetual Adoration shelter on June 9, 1962. Many of the other smaller stops on the North Shore Line had shelters just like this. Some stations were flag stops, meaning the train would not even bother to stop if no one was visible waiting to get on and no one signaled the conductor to get off.

Coaches Nos. 701 and 719 are part of an attractive winter night scene at the Mundelein Terminal in 1960. (Both, Robert Heinlein collection.)

Here is how the Mundelein Terminal looked on April 15, 1962. Insull staff architect Arthur U. Gerber designed three such buildings for the North Shore Line in three different sizes—small (Mundelein, 1926), medium (Kenosha, 1922), and large (Dempster, 1926). Of these, one is intact (Dempster), one has been altered with an addition (Kenosha), and Mundelein was demolished. Here, car No. 160 awaits its next departure. Now the second-oldest surviving North Shore coach, it is at the Illinois Railway Museum. (Marty Bernard photograph.)

The old North Shore Line Terminal in Mundelein was located on Prospect Avenue (shown here) just south of Hawley Street. The tracks were located between the two sets of poles, and the station was just to the right of the telephone poles. This photograph was taken on May 6, 2022.

This view is looking east from the west end of the Mundelein branch on May 15, 1960. West of the station, there were storage tracks for coaches and an interchange connection with the Soo Line. Much of the North Shore's freight business came via other railroads, and NSL sometimes acted as a "bridge," shuttling freight between two different railroads. (William C. Hoffman photograph.)

Commuter rail service returned to Mundelein on August 19, 1996, thirty-three years after the North Shore abandonment, with the opening of Metra's North Central line. A new brick station building was completed the following year, with a few visual cues that pay homage to the North Shore Line's old Mundelein Terminal, built in 1926. That station, long since demolished, was only a short distance east of here. This picture was taken on March 12, 2022.

Six

On the "L"

This 1940s map shows the locations of Loop "L" stations, relative to the various commuter rail terminals in downtown Chicago. While the North Shore Line cars ran very fast, they also made a lot more stops than the Milwaukee Road and Chicago & North Western limited express trains. Those trains were up to 25 minutes faster than the interurban, but the NSL had one other advantage—better distribution downtown. The Loop was unidirectional then, going counterclockwise. Since NSL trains terminated at Roosevelt Road (1200 South), riders on the Loop could not get on and off at the same stops. Fortunately, stops were close together. Northbound NSL trains used the Wabash and Lake sides of the Loop, while southbound trains went via Wabash and Van Buren.

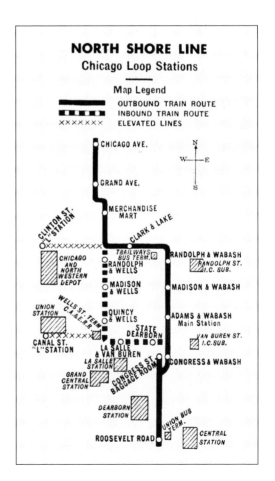

North Shore Line car No. 255 is laying over on the middle storage track at the Roosevelt Road station on the Chicago "L." No. 255 was built by the Jewett Car Company in 1917. All the seats were removed in the 1920s to create a full-length baggage car, which could run in passenger trains. This car was used to transport the Chicago Symphony Orchestra's instruments to Ravinia Park and sailor's baggage from Great Lakes. Seats were reinstalled for a time during World War II. (C. Edward Hedstrom Jr. photograph.)

This is an overhead view of Eighth Street, south of the Loop, on June 2, 1960. The head North Shore Line car is No. 420, built by Pullman in 1928 as an observation car. Out of service by 1932, it was rebuilt as a motorized coach in 1943. After abandonment, No. 420 went to the Seashore Trolley Museum in Maine. (Robert F. Collins photograph.)

A new Electroliner is shown above in the early 1940s. While the North Shore Line was in receivership in the 1930s, its competition was not idle. Both the Milwaukee Road and the Chicago & North Western introduced high-speed, limited-stop trains between Chicago and Milwaukee (the *Hiawatha* and *Twin Cities No. 400* , respectively). The interurban met its competitors with two streamlined, fast, air-conditioned cars of its own—the Electroliners. They were built between 1939 and 1941 by the St. Louis Car Company, the low bidder at $299,000 (ultimate cost: $310,000). The railroad paid one-third in cash, and the remainder in receiver's certificates, to be paid from future earnings. Both entered regular service on February 9, 1941, making five daily round trips—and an occasional sixth on Sunday evenings during World War II.

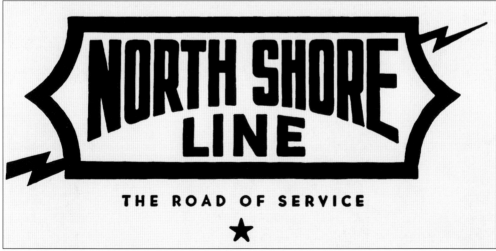

The North Shore Line used this logo in 1942, when World War II had just started. The railroad, newly energized with the addition of the two new modern Electroliners the previous year, did much for the war effort, as it served both Fort Sheridan and the Great Lakes Naval Base. Ridership swelled, in part due to gasoline and tire rationing and the complete shutdown of automobile production for the duration of the war. Success in the war years carried the interurban out of bankruptcy in 1946 but this did not continue, in large part due to the rapid demobilization at war's end.

Adams Street and Wabash Avenue was the North Shore Line's primary station on the Loop "L," and pictured here is a northbound train, led by combine No. 254, probably around 1939. A combine had fewer seats than a regular coach and had a section devoted to carrying baggage. The North Shore had a station in a building adjacent to the "L," with a direct second-floor walkway, ticket agent, and waiting room. (Gordon E. Lloyd photograph.)

On July 30, 1953, a northbound North Shore Line train departs from the Randolph Street station on Wabash Avenue, about to turn onto Lake Street. This photograph was taken from an upper floor at the nearby Marshall Field and Company department store. (Glenn S. Moe photograph.)

NSL cars Nos. 150 and 160 are heading west at the old Clark and Lake "L" station on Chicago's Loop on a January 12, 1963, railfan trip sponsored by the Central Electric Railfans' Association. Trains on the Loop ran in a counterclockwise direction on both tracks from 1913 to 1969. (William C. Hoffman photograph.)

On June 26, 1960, car No. 748 is southbound on Wells and Lake Streets, passing the original Tower No. 18. No. 748 was built by Pullman in 1928 and modernized in 1940. The NSL modernized 48 cars between 1939 and 1941. This was once the busiest railroad junction in the world before the opening of Chicago's subways. At peak times, nearly 1,000 cars might pass this spot in one hour. (Raymond DeGroote Jr. photograph.)

Car No. 181 heads up a northbound train at Chicago Avenue (800 North) on June 25, 1958. The "L" expanded out to four tracks just north of this station, and this continued almost continuously to Howard Street. North Shore trains were generally routed on the outer tracks.

North Shore Line's Nos. 727 and 729 are northbound at Belmont Avenue on the CTA north side "L" on May 20, 1962. No. 727 was built by the Cincinnati Car Company in 1926 and modernized in 1939. It has been at a few locations since 1963, all in Iowa. It is currently at the Iowa Traction Railway, the last remaining electric interurban freight operation in the country, where it occasionally runs.

A southbound train, led by car No. 709, prepares to stop at the North Shore–only platform at Belmont Avenue (3200 North) in Chicago. Starting in 1953, the Chicago Transit Authority made NSL trains stop here, to prevent their riders from transferring to the "L" without paying a CTA fare. Once one got off the train, he or she had to exit down to street level and come back up again through the CTA station if a transfer was needed. (John V. Engleman photograph.)

A southbound Electroliner is at the North Shore Line platform at Belmont Avenue. The conductor signals that everyone has cleared the doors. (Lee Hastman photograph/collection, 2010.030.C.03.116, Lake States Railway Historical Association, Baraboo, Wisconsin.)

A northbound Electroliner approaches the Wilson Avenue "L" station (4600 North) in the early 1950s. The North Shore Line maintained a ticket office there in what was called Uptown Union station.

North Shore Line Silverliners Nos. 770, 738, and 767 are just north of Wilson Avenue on June 2, 1962, crossing Broadway. This three-car train of Silverliners does not qualify as a "Substitute Liner" as it does not have dining car No. 415 in the consist. When the Electroliners were in the shop for regularly scheduled maintenance, No. 415 and two other Silverliners took their place.

On June 30, 1962, Raymond DeGroote Jr. captured this action shot of a southbound Electroliner at the Loyola Avenue curve, while a northbound train of CTA 6000-series cars passes.

North Shore Line No. 714 heads up a northbound train at the Loyola Avenue curve on July 13, 1955. It was built by the Cincinnati Car Company in 1926 and modernized in 1939. Car No. 714 is now at the Illinois Railway Museum.

On a snowy January 19, 1963, a southbound two-car North Shore Line train has just left the Howard Street (7600 North) "L" station on its way downtown. (Raymond DeGroote Jr. photograph.)

The conductor of a southbound North Shore Line train checks to make sure departing passengers have cleared the doors at Howard Street on June 2, 1962. (John Gruber photograph 04-34-049, Collection of the Center for Railroad Photography & Art.)

An Electroliner heads south from the Howard Street "L" station in June 1960. Note the trolley pole is raised, as a third rail was not installed on this track until the 1970s.

A northbound three-car Shore Line train has stopped at Main Street on the CTA Evanston "L" branch on July 8, 1955. Car No. 741, built by Pullman in 1928, was modernized in 1940. Note the extra set of southbound tracks here, which allowed electric freight trains to clear the station platform. (William C. Hoffman photograph.)

An Electroliner made an unusual appearance at the CTA "L" station at Fortieth Street and Indiana Avenue on a June 25, 1961, railfan trip. While North Shore trains did run on the South Side "L" from 1922 to 1938, that is before the Electroliners were introduced. They never ran south of Roosevelt Road in regular service. (Nick Jenkins photograph.)

North Shore Line car No. 251 crosses the bridge over the Illinois Central tracks on a May 15, 1960, railfan trip, approaching the terminal at Sixty-third Street and Stony Island Avenue on the CTA Jackson Park branch. North Shore Line trains were occasionally routed to the south side from 1922 until 1938; although, Roosevelt Road was always the main terminal. (William C. Hoffman photograph.)

Silverliner No. 409 is at Sixty-third Street and Stony Island Avenue, the then terminus of the CTA Jackson Park "L," on a Central Electric Railfans' Association railfan trip on May 15, 1960. The old Tower Theater, one of Chicago's great lost movie palaces, is visible in the distance. It opened in 1926, with a capacity of just under 3,000, as part of the Lubliner and Trinz theater chain. It closed in 1956 and was demolished soon after this picture was taken. (Raymond DeGroote Jr. photograph.)

Seven

CITY STREETCARS

The North Shore Line ran local streetcar service in Waukegan from its inception in the 1890s until 1947. By then, tracks and streetcars needed replacement, and the city wanted expanded service. Buses replaced streetcars, and the railroad spun this off into the Waukegan-North Chicago Transit Company, which was sold after the 1963 abandonment. Service in Waukegan continues today under Pace, a division of the six-county Regional Transportation Authority.

The North Shore Line had but a single streetcar line in Milwaukee, which competed against the Transport Company's Route 16. Shown here is one at Sixth Street and Oklahoma Avenue. A NSL Birney car is on the embankment. Many people would climb the stairs to ride the North Shore "Dinky," as they called it, to save a penny or two on the fare, compared to the Milwaukee streetcar. The Dinky fare was just a nickel, and it was faster than the competition, as part of the trip was on private right-of-way. The NSL route terminated at Second Street and Wisconsin Avenue in downtown Milwaukee. No timetables have been found, but service seems to have run about every 10 minutes. (Bob Genack photograph; Larry Sakar collection.)

City streetcar No. 506 is in North Chicago on July 25, 1947, about four months before buses replaced trolleys. It was built by the St. Louis Car Company in 1909 and scrapped in 1948.

Here is North Shore Line Birney car No. 336 in Milwaukee in 1946. The Chicago & Milwaukee Electric, predecessor of the CNS&M, remained the franchise holder, so that is how the cars were lettered until the end of streetcar service in 1951. The Birneys were retired in 1947, after Waukegan streetcar service ended, and the equipment used there was shifted to Milwaukee. No. 336 was built by the Cincinnati Car Company in December 1922 and scrapped in April 1948.

North Shore Line city streetcar No. 354 heads south on Sixth Street at National Avenue in July 1951, a month before buses replaced streetcars in Milwaukee. No. 354 was built by the St. Louis Car Company in January 1928. It made the last run on August 12, 1951, and was then sold to the Chicago Hardware Foundry in North Chicago. Eventually, it was acquired by the Illinois Railway Museum, where it remains.

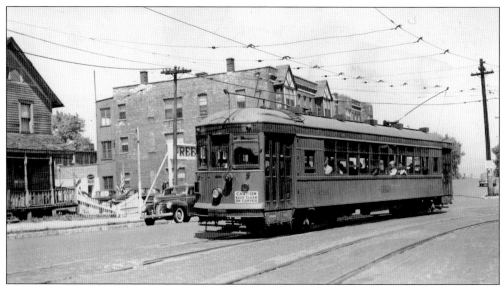

North Shore Line city streetcar No. 356 navigates "Merchant's Curve" in Waukegan during the 1940s. The photographer was standing on the south side of Belvidere Street looking east/northeast. This westbound streetcar is turning off Marion Street (now South Genesee Street) and will soon turn right onto South Genesee Street, as it travels north through the center of downtown Waukegan. The sailors visible in the car are heading to downtown Waukegan from Great Lakes Naval Base, the south end of the line.

Several North Shore Line wooden coaches were leased to the Chicago Aurora & Elgin from 1936 to 1945. They returned to the railroad briefly before being sold outright to the CA&E. Just before they left the property for the last time, Central Electric Railfans' Association used cars Nos. 130 and 139 on a July 14, 1946, railfan trip. It is seen here in Waukegan on the Franklin Street siding between County Street and North Avenue. North Elementary School is at left. These tracks were used by Waukegan streetcars until they were replaced by buses on November 16, 1947.

North Shore Line streetcar No. 313 is shown operating in downtown Waukegan, most likely during the early 1930s. It was originally built by the St. Louis Car Company in 1915 for the Empire State Railway for service in Oswego, New York. The North Shore Line purchased it in 1918 and had it rebuilt for one-man service. It was retired in 1941 and scrapped in 1945. As far as is known, it never operated in Milwaukee.

Waukegan streetcar No. 357 is on County Street near Washington Street in 1946. The riders probably came from the Lake County Courthouse, located just out of view to the left. Car No. 357 was built by the St. Louis Car Company in January 1928. It briefly was used in Milwaukee, after Waukegan streetcar service ended in 1947, but was scrapped in 1950.

Chicago and Milwaukee Electric Birney car No. 332 is at the north end of the line on Second Street and Wisconsin Avenue in Milwaukee around 1940. This was the original terminus (1908–1920) of North Shore Line interurbans in Milwaukee, prior to the opening of the off-street terminal. City streetcars continued to run to this location per franchise requirements until 1950, when service was cut back to the Milwaukee Terminal before being abandoned altogether in 1951. Notice there was no track connection here with the Milwaukee Electric's tracks on Wisconsin Avenue, but C&ME did share three blocks of its trackage on Wells Street with other streetcars. This view is looking north. (Bill Becwar collection.)

Eight

TROLLEY FREIGHT

Baggage is loaded and unloaded from a northbound North Shore Line train at the Kenosha station in June 1962. The interurban was often the quickest way to get small packages to various points along its route. (Ed Wilkommen photograph/collection, 2018.15.SM.242-08, Lake States Railway Historical Association, Baraboo, Wisconsin.)

Once North Shore Line trains began running on the "L" in 1919, they needed a convenient place to load and unload baggage downtown. The solution was to use the old Congress Terminal, located a short distance north of the Roosevelt Road station. This had been the original terminal of the South Side "L" but was used less and less by such trains as the years went by. From 1949 until 1963, the interurban had exclusive use of the facility. Pictured here is car No. 742 in the early 1950s.

In 1926, the North Shore Line pioneered the development of trailer-on-flatcar freight service, now popularly known as piggyback. This extended the range of what the railroad could carry, since trucks could now bring it here and take it there. The new service was made possible by the opening of the Skokie Valley Route. This picture shows a North Shore piggyback train, powered by Merchandise Despatch cars. Ultimately, the interurban faced too much competition from truckers and other railroads, who developed piggyback services of their own, and discontinued trailer-on-flatcar services on April 30, 1947. (J.J. Sedelmaier collection.)

Locomotive No. 456 is running freight in North Chicago on March 2, 1946. No. 456 was built by General Electric in 1927. It and locomotive No. 455 had banks of batteries installed and could operate for five miles without overhead wire if needed. The smaller locomotives were nicknamed the "Pups." (Gordon E. Lloyd photograph.)

North Shore Line No. 458 heads up a southbound freight train in Waukegan, between Washington and Cornelia Streets, in the early 1950s. The building at right was a former North Shore Line Merchandise Despatch station, by this time being rented out to a produce dealer. The NSL purchased this 1941-vintage electric locomotive in 1947 from the Oregon Electric Railway.

Merchandise Despatch car No. 215 poses at the Harrison Street Shops in Milwaukee on July 7, 1953. It was built by Cincinnati Car Company in October 1922 and was eventually de-motorized and used as a tool car.

A pair of CTA "curved door" Presidents' Conference Committee (PCC) rapid transit cars is being delivered to Skokie Shops via the North Shore Line in the 1950s. These used parts were salvaged from scrapped Chicago PCC streetcars. This is an example of the North Shore functioning as a "bridge," bringing freight from one railroad to another. These cars were built by the St. Louis Car Company and may have traveled partway via the Illinois Terminal Railroad.

Locomotive No. 455 hauls a freight train near Great Lakes on the one remaining Shore Line Route track in July 1962. (William C. Hoffman photograph.)

Caboose No. 1003 brings up the rear of an eastbound freight train on the Mundelein branch on May 30, 1962. The railroad bought No. 1003 new in 1926. It went to the Illinois Railway Museum in 1963. (William C. Hoffman photograph.)

After Samuel Insull took control of the North Shore Line in 1916, the railroad developed a less-than-carload freight business. Merchandise Despatch stations were established, like this one at 1040 West Montrose Avenue (4400 North) in Chicago, where a nearby interchange existed between the "L" and the Milwaukee Road. The North Shore gave up on this business in 1947, as there was too much competition from trucking. Here is how the station looked on November 11, 1939. (Gordon E. Lloyd photograph.)

North Shore freight locomotive No. 451 was built in 1907 by Alco and General Electric. It was retired in 1948 and scrapped the following year. Here, it is pictured at the Buena Yard in Chicago, an interchange point between the Northwestern "L" and the Milwaukee Road. Behind No. 451, one can see the ramp that went from ground level up to the "L." A Merchandise Despatch car is also visible. It is not clear what No. 451 would be doing here unless it was needed to haul piggyback freight. The Chicago Rapid Transit Company had two electric locomotives of its own, which picked up freight from the Milwaukee Road and delivered it to customers along the "L."

The North Shore Line repainted four Merchandise Despatch cars (including No. 212, seen here) to promote the sales of war bonds during World War II. Much of the railroad's huge increase in business during the war, both passenger and freight, was related to the war effort. Once Insull took over the North Shore Line, he purchased a fleet of Merchandise Despatch cars with dimensions and a profile like that of the passenger cars. These were useful to carry less-than-carload freight in places where it would otherwise have been prohibited by local ordinance. These became work cars after the railroad got out of that business in 1947.

On June 14, 1962, North Shore electric locomotive No. 459 heads up a freight train in Lake Bluff. (Jeffrey L. Wien photograph.)

North Shore Line freight locomotive No. 456 and caboose No. 1002 are at the scale house in Rondout on the Mundelein branch during January 1963.

Locomotive No. 459 and caboose No. 1006 are at Lake Bluff on a snowy January 19, 1963. (Raymond DeGroote Jr. photograph.)

Merchandise Despatch cars were infrequent visitors on the "L" but sometimes brought supplies to the interurban's facilities at Roosevelt Road. Pictured is Merchandise Despatch car No. 235 on March 8, 1951, heading northbound on Wabash Avenue in the Loop. The Epicurean Restaurant, seen at left, was located at 316 South Wabash Avenue. (William E. Robertson photograph; Eric Bronsky collection.)

North Shore Line electric locomotive No. 456 heads up a short freight train in North Chicago on January 20, 1963—the last full day of operations prior to abandonment.

Nine

THE LONG GOODBYE

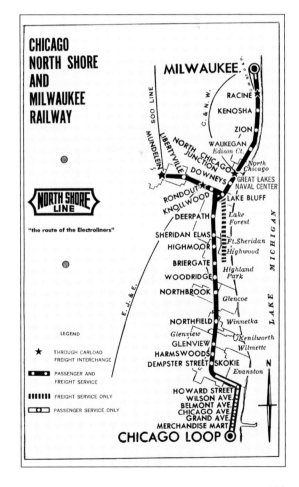

This map shows where the North Shore Line operated from 1955 until 1963. Passenger service had been abandoned on the Shore Line Route, but one track was retained on a portion of it for use by freight and for access to the Highwood Shops.

Coach No. 730 is at North Chicago Junction in August 1960. (Jeffrey L. Wien photograph.)

Silverliner No. 758 is at Edison Court in Waukegan during the fall of 1958. This was an important stop, where cars were regularly added and cut. Headlights on these train cars were not permanently attached, and the crew appears to be adding one to the front of this southbound car.

Once the North Shore Line filed for abandonment of its remaining lines in 1958, fans came out to see, ride, and document the NSL, right up until the last car ran in 1963. Decades later, many of the younger fans are still fans of the railroad. The young man in this picture may be collecting Social Security now, but chances are he still remembers this train, this place, this moment. The work of historic preservation is never really finished; it is ongoing in railroad museums, libraries, historical societies, and private collections. It is a gift preservationists give to future generations.

On February 19, 1956, a northbound Electroliner has stopped at Kenosha and is presumably on a fantrip, as a leisurely photo stop seems to be underway. (William C. Hoffman photograph.)

Southbound Electroliner No. 803–804 is at speed at Green Bay Road in Lake Bluff on May 30, 1962. (William C. Hoffman photograph.)

William A. Steventon of Hawkins, Wisconsin, made many audio recordings of train sounds and released several LPs through his Railroad Record Club. Here, he is using a portable tape recorder. His North Shore Line recordings were made between 1956 and 1960. These have been reissued on compact discs. Stanwood C. Griffith, Brad Miller, and David A. Myers Jr. also made such recordings. Only Griffith captured the sounds of the Shore Line Route, documenting the stop-and-go nature of that operation.

The North Shore Line emphasized safety to its employees, but sometimes accidents were unavoidable. Car No. 166 was heading up a fast four-car train at Lake-Cook Road on January 24, 1959, when a driver went around the crossing gates to get ahead of a slow C&NW freight train on adjacent tracks. The driver failed to heed the approaching train's frantic whistle, and a collision was unavoidable. The driver was killed instantly, and the lead car derailed, hit a catenary support column, and rolled over into a ditch. The other three cars remained on the tracks. The driver was the sole fatality. The demolished car was brought back to Pettibone Yards, where William C. Hoffman took this picture on February 15, prior to scrapping.

The unrestored interior of car No. 151 is shown here on September 4, 1961. The original coal-burning stove is at left toward the front of the car. This car was built by Brill in 1915. (William C. Hoffman photograph.)

While the North Shore did modernize many of their cars, there were still some that were never upgraded at the end of service. Here, one sees car No. 151's coal-burning stove on September 4, 1961. David A. Myers Jr. owns a similar stove that was taken out of car No. 150 while it was being scrapped. To get it out, the roof had to be removed first. (William C. Hoffman photograph.)

On February 20, 1961, Chicago mayor Richard J. Daley sent the following telegram: "At the suggestion of many people in the metropolitan area—including some of the mayors—I am calling a meeting in my office for Thursday, February 23, at 2:30 p.m. to discuss the projected abandonment of the North Shore Railroad and the possibility of initiating a mass transportation authority for the metropolitan area. I do hope you can arrange your schedule to be in attendance and will appreciate your calling my office Randolph 6-8000 extension 304 to indicate whether or not you will be here." Several local officials did attend the February 23 meeting, but it took until 1974 to create the six-county Regional Transportation Authority that helped save Chicago's commuter rail network. (History Center of Lake Forest-Lake Bluff collection, 2012.4.1.)

Photographer Bruce Meyer caught an Electroliner passing a Chicago & North Western *Twin Cities No. 400* train at Lake Bluff in November 1962. The C&NW was a much larger railroad than the North Shore Line and therefore had resources for upgrading and modernizing its equipment that were not available to the interurban. C&NW replaced steam locomotives with diesels in 1956 and now had a fleet of air-conditioned bi-levels. The NSL was losing customers to its competitor as a result and cited this as one of the reasons for abandonment. (Bruce Meyer photograph/collection, 2018.008.CNSM.I.081, Lake States Railway Historical Association, Baraboo, Wisconsin.)

A Chicago & North Western train of bi-levels is at the Milwaukee station on the lakefront in 1962. The railroad operated a limited-stop train called the *Twin Cities No. 400* between Chicago, Milwaukee, and Minneapolis-St. Paul from 1935 until July 23, 1963, just six months after the North Shore abandonment. Local service to Milwaukee continued through April 30, 1971, after which it was cut back to Kenosha.

The photographer (possibly Emery Gulash) had but one chance to press the shutter button at precisely the right moment, and he nailed it with this classic view of northbound Electroliner train No. 803–804 crossing Illinois 176 in Lake Bluff during January 1963. This is what noted photographer Henri Cartier-Bresson had in mind when he wrote about the "decisive moment."

Although the final date for abandonment had already been set and approved in May 1962, the North Shore Line still managed to refurbish the interior of car No. 160 in November of that year, just two months before the shutdown. That just goes to show how dedicated the railroad's employees were to maintaining service and standards, all the way until the end. Raymond DeGroote took this picture on January 12, 1963.

With the announcement in May 1962 that the interurban would soon be no more, a flurry of railfan trips ensued, and fans came out in droves to take pictures. This unusual sight shows two railfan trip trains side by side on the Mundelein branch in June 1962. (Jim Martin photograph.)

The Omnibus Society of America held a railfan trip on September 23, 1962, using Waukegan-North Chicago Transit Company bus No. 25. The bus is posed here at Scranton Avenue in Lake Bluff, along with North Shore Silverliners Nos. 761 and 760. After the abandonment, the bus company was sold off. (Raymond DeGroote Jr. photograph.)

Starting in 1958, the North Shore Commuters' Association (NSCA) kept up a determined, if ultimately quixotic, fight to save the interurban. While it only raised a fraction of the money needed to purchase the railroad, much less modernize it, the group's efforts helped postpone abandonment for four years. It also paved the way for later, more successful efforts to save Chicago's commuter rail system and the South Shore Line. William C. Hoffman documented this NSCA sign at the Waukegan station on January 12, 1963.

Howard Odinius (1917–1973) is at the controls of an Electroliner in October 1962. He was one of the original 10 founders of the Illinois Railway Museum in 1953. Odinius began working for the North Shore Line in 1939 and was still there at the end. After the line quit, he spent the rest of his career at the Milwaukee Road. (Ed Wilkommen photograph/collection, 2018.15.SM.264-013, Lake States Railway Historical Association, Baraboo, Wisconsin.)

The final North Shore railfan trip took place on January 12, 1963, using unrestored cars Nos. 150 and 160, both built by Brill in 1915. A photo stop took place at Kostner on the Skokie Valley Route, where there was a closed station, last used in 1948, from the old Chicago Rapid Transit Company's Nile Center "L" branch. The station was never used by the North Shore Line but was designed by Insull staff architect Arthur U. Gerber and bore many similarities to interurban stations he created. It was a successful combination of Prairie-style and Bungalow Vernacular architecture. A photographer from *Life* magazine accompanied this trip. The station was torn down in 1964, shortly after the CTA Skokie Swift began running, as it interfered with grade crossing visibility for the high-speed cars. (William C. Hoffman photograph.)

A southbound Electroliner crosses under the Elgin, Joliet & Eastern Railway at speed in North Chicago on January 12, 1963, a little over a week before the end of service.

Looking east from the Milwaukee Terminal on the chilly last full day of service (January 20, 1963), one sees Silverliner No. 773, which ran that night as part of the last southbound train. It looks as though someone has swiped the car's metal herald. (William C. Hoffman photograph.)

On January 20, 1963, the last night in Milwaukee, a man buys ticket while a fan watches. (John Gruber photograph 05-03-385, Collection of the Center for Railroad Photography & Art.)

This and the following picture show the lunch counter at the Milwaukee Terminal on January 20, 1963, the final night. (John Gruber photographs 05-03-376 and 05-03-321, Collection of the Center for Railroad Photography & Art.)

One of the last southbound Electroliners prepares to leave the Milwaukee Terminal on January 20, 1963. (John V. Engleman photograph.)

An Electroliner at Roosevelt Road on a very cold January 20, 1963, is seen next to cars stored on the middle track. (John V. Engleman photograph.)

John V. Engleman took this picture of what may have been the very last Electroliner to reach Roosevelt Road on the evening of January 20, 1963.

The last southbound train arrived at Howard Street at 2:35 a.m. on January 21, 1963, with car No. 720 in the lead. It ran late due to the large number of people on board and the cold weather. No. 720 was built by the Cincinnati Car Company in 1926. It was damaged in the North Shore Line's worst-ever accident on February 23, 1930, in Kenosha. It was rebuilt and later modernized in 1939. (LeRoy Blommaert collection.)

William Henry Livings (1911–1966) and Henry Joseph Bondy (1918–2005) crewed the final train. Motorman Livings piloted southbound run No. 436 to Roosevelt Road, with cars Nos. 720, 763, 766, and 738 (plus Nos. 773 and 252, which only went as far as Waukegan). Conductor Bondy called out the last stop at 2:54 a.m. on a very frigid January 21, 1963, morning, with temperatures reaching minus 20°F, and the North Shore Line had finally made its last run. (Above, Robert Heinlein collection; below, Charles L. Tauscher photograph.)

David A. Myers Jr. rode the last northbound North Shore Line train as far north as Edison Court and brought a portable tape recorder with him. He is shown here while taking that very chilly ride. It is thanks to the tireless dedication and foresight of Myers and his father that many of the documents and artifacts of the railroad were saved. His father worked for the railroad as an executive for more than 40 years, and David A. Myers Jr. had various jobs there, including as a car washer and working in the shops. Even when officials offered them items for free, they insisted on paying for everything and getting receipts. People can be very thankful for their service to future generations in preserving the history of the North Shore Line.

The last trains on an abandoned railroad are referred to as "clean-up trains," as they go around removing stray pieces of equipment along the line. Here, on January 21, 1963, locomotive No. 456 heads south at Lake Bluff on what had previously been the northbound track. The last such move occurred at 2:10 p.m. on January 25, when locomotive No. 455 pulled into the yard. (Robert Heinlein photograph.)

This photograph, showing a mirror at the North Shore Line's Milwaukee Terminal, was taken after abandonment on January 21, 1963, by Allan Y. Scott for the *Milwaukee Journal* using a Leica M2 or M3 camera.

Here is how the Milwaukee Terminal's interior looked on May 30, 1963, four months after it closed. The building was leveled the following year. (William C. Hoffman photograph.)

A group of steel coaches awaits its appointment with the scrapper at Lake Bluff in 1963. They remained there for many months before their inevitable demise. (Robert Heinlein photograph.)

Silverliner No. 766 goes up in flames on January 5, 1964. Cars were set on fire, sometimes a few at one time. After the combustible parts had burned up, the remaining metal was salvaged and hauled away by train. The work was done near an interchange point with another railroad. The practice of burning old transit cars ended around 1981, as it polluted the air. (David A. Myers Jr. photograph.)

Silverliner No. 737 was torched by Hyman-Michaels, a scrapper, on December 21, 1963. One sees it here on Christmas Day at Rondout on the Mundelein branch. (Jeffrey L. Wien photograph.)

The remains of scrapped locomotive No. 452 are at Rondout, while three coaches, including No. 410, wait their turn. No. 452 was scrapped on February 21, 1964, while No. 410 was destroyed the following day. (David A. Myers Jr. photograph.)

North Shore Line snowplow No. 605 had a metal plow but was mostly built out of wood by the Russell Car and Snow Plow Company in 1921. It ended up being the last piece of NSL equipment scrapped on the property. According to David A. Myers Jr., he found someone willing to save the plow, but they procrastinated so long that eventually all the tracks were torn up around it, so there was no way to move it. Here is how it looked at Pettibone Yard on July 25, 1964, when its days were numbered. (Jeffrey L. Wien photograph.)

In February 1964, car No. 727 has been loaded on a flatcar at Pettibone Yard in North Chicago for transport to the Iowa Chapter of the National Railway Historical Society. The car has bounced around to a few locations but has remained in Iowa. It is now at the Iowa Traction Railway, headquartered in Mason City. (Ed Wilkommen photograph/collection, 2018.15.N99B.7645, Lake States Railway Historical Association, Baraboo, Wisconsin.)

Rails are being removed on the line south of Woodridge on June 29, 1965. (Jeffrey L. Wien photograph.)

Both Electroliners were sold to the Philadelphia Suburban Transportation Company in 1963 and shipped there in November, where David H. Cope took this picture of the new arrival. One sees a Bullet car at right, built in 1931 by Brill for the Philadelphia & Western Railroad. The Bullets were the first streamlined electric railcars and were designed using a wind tunnel. Capable of speeds up to 90 miles per hour, they were to some extent a forerunner of the Electroliners.

A sign painter applies the finishing touches to one of the new Liberty Liners at the Philadelphia Suburban Transportation Company on January 4, 1964. This private operator branded itself as the Red Arrow Lines from 1936 until it was purchased by the Southeastern Pennsylvania Transportation Authority in 1970. Operations had been halted by a 34-day strike in 1963, and company president Merritt H. Taylor Jr. (1922–2010) bought the two former Electroliners, in part, to restore goodwill with the public. (David H. Cope photograph.)

The two Electroliners were purchased by the Philadelphia Suburban Transportation Company (also known as Red Arrow Lines) in 1963 and were reconfigured into Liberty Liners. Liners Nos. 801–802, seen here, became the *Valley Forge* and Nos. 803–804, the *Independence Hall*. Jeffrey L. Wien took this photograph at their introduction on January 26, 1964, a little over a year since they last ran in Chicago.

One of the two Liberty Liners is seen on April 5, 1964, at the elevated Norristown Terminal of the Red Arrow Lines' former Philadelphia & Western Railway line, which is approximately 13 miles long. The former Electroliners did not turn out to be a perfect fit here, as stops were closely spaced, and the cars were only able to do about 60 miles per hour. (Jeffrey L. Wien photograph.)

The Chicago Transit Authority purchased five miles of the Skokie Valley Route after the North Shore Line quit in 1963. Half of this was needed to reach CTA's Skokie Shops. Skokie agreed to help subsidize the cost of resuming "L" service to Dempster Street, and the CTA also received some funding from the federal government as a demonstration project. A large parking lot was built, and service began on the new Skokie Swift on April 20, 1964. The CTA modified four existing high-speed cars for use on this express service. Here, one sees car No. 2 in the 1960s. The service was successful beyond all expectations and has since become a permanent route—the CTA Yellow Line.

Chicago Transit Authority's high-speed single-car unit No. 1 is at the Skokie Swift's Dempster Terminal on June 11, 1965, just over a year since the service began. These cars could go 65 miles per hour at a time when the "L" fleet was only capable of 45 to 50. They paved the way for the faster "L" cars of today.

This July 2, 1964, view is looking north along the former North Shore Line right-of-way at Dempster Street, just north of where the CTA Skokie Swift ends. The Chicago & North Western Railway purchased the tracks between here and Lake-Cook Road, several miles to the north. The southbound track was retained for freight use and replaced the C&NW's dilapidated line just west of here. When William C. Hoffman took this picture, the overhead wires had already been removed, but the connection to the C&NW had not yet been built.

Having taken over service on a portion of the former North Shore right-of-way, Chicago & North Western diesel locomotive No. 1099 runs freight cars over to the Great Lakes Naval Base on August 5, 1964. (Jeffrey L. Wien photograph.)

This is how the former Mundelein branch right-of-way looked going west from St. Mary's Road in January 1964. (Jeffrey L. Wien photograph.)

The North Shore Line's Milwaukee Terminal, built in 1920, was demolished during the summer of 1964.

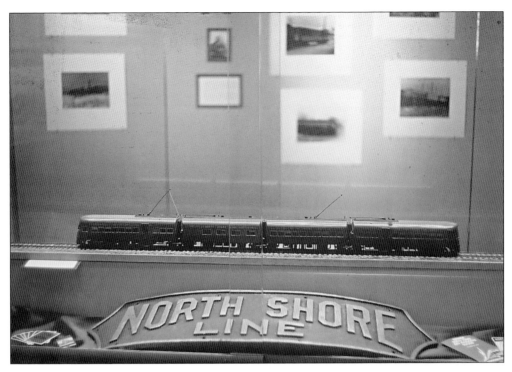

The Racine County Historical Society Museum exhibited many artifacts and memorabilia on April 2, 1966, in an exhibit called The End of An Era: The Chicago North Shore & Milwaukee. Items belonging to David A. Myers Jr. were displayed, including this original herald from Electroliners Nos. 803–804 and the dispatcher's desk (below). (Roger Puta photographs; Marty Bernard collection.)

Ten

THE LEGACY

A modern Milwaukee streetcar, branded as "The Hop," passes the Milwaukee Public Market as it heads west on East St. Paul Avenue in the historic Third Ward on June 7, 2019. The 2.1-mile initial line uses the first electric railcars to run on Milwaukee's streets since the North Shore Line's demise in 1963.

While the North Shore Line is but a fond memory, the South Shore Line still exists and is undergoing a remarkable transformation in 2022. Earlier that year, after 114 years, street running in Michigan City came to an end, and the tracks there are being relocated onto private right-of-way. The entire line is being double-tracked, and eventually a new branch line to Dyer, Indiana, will be built. Metra will lease 26 Metra Electric "Highliners" to the Northern Indiana Commuter Transportation District to provide service on the new branch. This September 3, 2022, photograph of the Beverly Shores, Indiana, station, taken by Scott Patrick, demonstrates the historical connections between the two Insull interurbans. This station building, dating to 1929, is nearly identical to nine that were constructed three years earlier on the Skokie Valley Route. But whereas the Beverly Shores station has been listed in the National Register of Historic Places since 1989, the former NSL Briergate station faces an uncertain future and may eventually be demolished. When the South Shore Line's owners petitioned to abandon passenger service in 1976, they cited many of the reasons the North Shore Line had in its 1958 petition. But in part due to the lessons learned from the NSL's demise, this time the public mobilized, and the South Shore Line was saved. More recently, the State of Indiana has recognized the interurban as an economic development engine and, in partnership with federal and local governments, is making significant investments in upgrading it. If the North Shore Line had survived, it would be considered just as indispensable today.

The North Shore Line's Milwaukee Terminal was a gateway to the downtown area for millions of riders. For many years, a large billboard advertised "38 Fast Trains Daily," or 19 round trips. In 2022, Amtrak offers seven daily round trips on its Hiawatha service between Chicago and Milwaukee, with one additional northbound run on Friday evenings. Silverliner 737 (at left) and "Greenliner" 767 (at right) prepare to depart on May 24, 1953. (Robert Selle photograph.)

In 1938, it cost $1.70 to ride from Roosevelt Road in Chicago to the Milwaukee Terminal, the equivalent of $35.71 in 2022. A one-way Amtrak ticket currently costs $25.

On September 24, 2021, concertgoers await the opening of the entrance to Ravinia Park, where they will hear a program by headliner Andrew Bird, with an opening set by the Flat Five. The Tyler Gate and the Martin Theater (visible in the background) are the only original structures that remain in the park, built in 1904 by the Chicago & Milwaukee Electric. On concert days, Metra offers commuter rail service direct to this spot via tracks adjacent to where the North Shore Line once ran.

One of the two large signs from the North Shore Line Milwaukee Terminal has been preserved at the Illinois Railway Museum in Union. It is pictured here on May 28, 2022.

A portion of the ticket window from the North Shore Line's Milwaukee Terminal has been incorporated into the depot at the Illinois Railway Museum in Union. A picture of the original ticket booth, which formed an octagonal island, can be found in chapter nine. This picture was taken on May 28, 2022.

The Briergate station, seen here on March 12, 2022, is the last survivor of nine nearly identical stations along the Skokie Valley Route. Built in 1926, it was designed by Arthur U. Gerber, an Insull staff architect, in a style that has come to be known as "Insull Spanish." A similar building, constructed in 1929, still exists on the South Shore Line at Beverly Shores, Indiana. That structure was added to the National Register of Historic Places in 1989, but the Briergate station's future is uncertain. The building is currently for rent, and a few years ago, the owners sought to demolish it.

Westleigh Road crosses the old Shore Line Route in Lake Forest via a 1946 underpass. The North Shore Line concrete sign was still intact on the east side of the bridge on March 12, 2022. The Robert McClory Bike Path follows the old North Shore right-of-way here. There was a nearby station stop for the Sacred Heart Academy starting in 1904.

On April 26, 2014, Chicago Transit Authority cars Nos. 5237–5238 are at Main Street in Skokie, running on the Yellow Line. Service on five miles of the Skokie Valley Route resumed in April 1964, just over a year since the North Shore abandonment. Third rail replaced overhead wire in September 2004, but many of the original 1926 catenary support bridges are still in place.

North Shore Line No. 727, built in 1926 and now nearly a century old, has no difficulty keeping up with Interstate 35 highway traffic along the Iowa Traction Railway on September 13, 2018. Engineer and general manager John Richards waves to photographer Marco Moerland.

Incredibly, nearly 60 years after the abandonment, there are still original North Shore Line rails to be found. In 1963, the Chicago & North Western purchased the tracks between Dempster and Lake-Cook Road and used a single track for freight. On May 7, 2002, the Union Pacific, successor to the Chicago & North Western, filed to discontinue service between those two points. Rails have been removed at the crossings and other locations but still exist in a few places. This section, pictured on May 30, 2022, is a short distance south of Lake-Cook Road and includes rail installed by the North Shore Line in 1926 and 1943.

Mitch Markovitz is an acclaimed artist who has also worked as a conductor and train operator. He has a special talent for creating highly realistic, evocative paintings of transit scenes from the past. He describes this as follows: "An illustration influenced by a North Shore Line brochure touting the road's limited trains, parlors, and diners, featuring *The Cream City Special*, the noon time limited from Sixty-third Street and Dorchester Avenue to Milwaukee that carried both a parlor and a diner. Two businessmen, Messieurs Harbin and Corbin each decide to take this train. One boards at Sixty-third Street, the other in the Loop. At Wilson Avenue they see a mutual friend board and go directly into the diner. They decide to join him for lunch." (Opaque watercolor on illustration board, private collection; courtesy of Mitch Markovitz.)

On June 27, 2021, the East Troy Railroad Museum dedicated newly restored Silverliner No. 761, the culmination of an extensive restoration project. Museum operations in East Troy began in 1972, and other North Shore cars have operated there, but the original group that ran the museum left and took its cars with them. It is only fitting that an original North Shore Line car should run in Wisconsin, since the railroad played such an important role in the state's history. Here is how the car looked on May 15, 2022.

The interior of newly restored car No. 761 is seen on May 15, 2022.

Electroliner Nos. 801–802 is undergoing a total restoration at the Illinois Railway Museum, where it has been since 1982. Volunteers Sam Sorenson (left) and Steve Sorenson (right) are shown working in the tavern/lounge car on June 5, 2022. Ed Oslowski is the interior project manager.

Renovation work is complete in Electroliner coach section A-1 (No. 802), seen here on June 5, 2022. The results are outstanding.

On August 29, 2021, Electroliner Nos. 801–802 posed for pictures on the streetcar loop at the Illinois Railway Museum. This was the first time in many years it was operated using all eight motors. Restoration work began in July 2013. The exterior work is done, but much work remains inside. By the time this million-dollar restoration project is finished, taking more than a decade, this Electroliner will be in like new condition. It is the pride and joy of the Illinois Railway Museum, a true "museum in motion." (Frank Hicks photograph.)

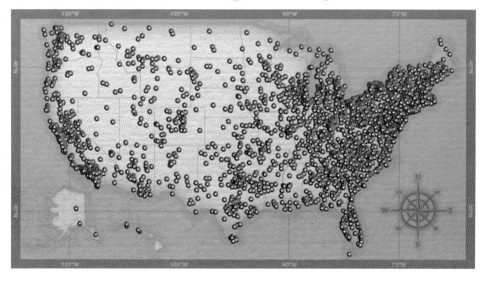